UNDECEIVED

UNDECEIVED

FROM AMISH TRADITION TO CHRIST'S REDEMPTION

ELI YODER

Edited by
BRIAN PAULES

Released: December 2024
ISBN: 978-1-64457-768-4

Rise UP Publications
www.riseUPpublications.com
Phone: 866-846-5123

To my beloved father, Henry Yoder:

Though you could not see the light beyond the shadows, you paved the way for mine. This book is for you, with love and in remembrance.

Having a form of godliness, but denying the power thereof: from such turn away.

2 TIMOTHY 3:5 (KJV)

CONTENTS

ACKNOWLEDGMENTS

First and foremost, I want to thank my father, Henry Yoder, whose life and struggles inspired this book. Though he is no longer with us, his struggles and resilience continue to guide me every day.

I am deeply grateful to my family and friends who have supported me through my journey. Your unwavering love and encouragement have been my anchor.

To my wife, who has always believed in me, and to my son, who deserved more from me than he received, thank you for your loving support.

A special thanks to my editor, Brian Paules, whose keen insights, and thoughtful suggestions have shaped this book into what it is today. Your dedication and hard work are deeply appreciated.

To my publisher, Rise Up Publications, who saw the potential in this story and helped bring it to life, thank you for your faith in this project.

Finally, to all the readers who pick up this book, thank you for taking the time to walk with me through my journey with Jesus. I pray this challenges you to live a life free from religious bondage, and that you are set free to live undeceived in Jesus' name.

INTRODUCTION

My life journey began in the heart of an Old-Order Amish community, amidst an oppressive and legalistic religious system and the challenges of having an alcoholic parent. I was caught between an existence I could not bear, and the expectation of eternal damnation for defying the Amish church ordinance. Now, as "The Preaching Truck driver," I live in Waynesfield, Ohio, with my wife Nikki and our son Johnathan. We serve the Lord together as a family, loving others and making an eternal difference in this world.

Undeceived is the story of my struggle and transformation. It's about my passage from the burden of deceptive traditions to a life illuminated by the truth of the Bible. This truth has set me free and drives my mission to help others break free from oppression and deception. In 2017, I experienced a life-changing encounter with Jesus when I felt His presence come over me. That moment marked a turning point, and from that day forward, I committed myself to following Jesus and sharing the truth with others. This journey has been tremendously rewarding, though not always easy.

I wrote this book to help people from all walks of life break free from traditions that deny or hide the truth and provide false security. None of us get to choose the traditions and beliefs we are born into. Our early traditions and beliefs shape how we see ourselves, the world, and what we believe to be true. As we grow and mature, we become responsible for examining and challenging the traditions imposed upon us as we walk the path from tradition to truth. This journey may be easy for some, but for others, it is a long and painful struggle.

Before I begin my story, I want to be very clear about something—this is not a tell-all book about Amish life intending to defame the Amish community at large. I am critical of specific Amish traditions where it is deserved, but my love and respect for the Amish people and their way of living have grown stronger with time. Most Amish are hardworking, honest, and deeply devoted to their families. The Amish are not like a religious denomination with one set of rules for all. The beliefs and traditions among Amish communities are quite diverse, and a growing number are breaking away from the harmful practices mentioned in this book. So, please don't judge every Amish person based on my personal experience.

People from all walks of life hold on to man-made religious traditions in an attempt to manage God. These traditions provide a false but addictive sense of superiority, security, and power, making people feel good about themselves while keeping them blind to the truth. This condition is not unique to my Old Order Amish community—it may be present in your life as well.

You may have grown up in a household following a different religious tradition, or perhaps none. Our starting points vary, but our need to free ourselves from the deceptions of our past remains the same. What we all truly seek is truth, not tradition.

Journey alongside me as I share my path to discovering the truth of Jesus in the Bible and the freedom I found. You may find some similarities between my story and your own. You might even look at your own life a bit differently afterward. I sincerely hope you are blessed, challenged, and encouraged by my story. But most of all, I hope you find freedom in the truth of Jesus as I have so that you can live an undeceived life.

PART 1

GROWING UP AMISH

1

THE BEGINNING

My journey began in an Old Order Amish community within the rural farmland of Hardin County, Ohio. It's a world of old traditions and deeply held religious beliefs. My maternal grandfather, Levi Beechy, held the highly respected position of bishop in our community. He wasn't just any bishop; he was the original bishop who established our tight-knit community in Kenton, Ohio back in 1951. The Kenton community was known for its strict adherence to the Articles of Faith written by Jakob Ammann, the founder of the Amish tradition. These Articles, known as the Ordnung, governed nearly every facet of our lives, and defined what it meant to be "Amish." To stray from these rules meant to risk shunning or even excommunication from the community, a fate we believed would lead to eternal damnation.

My parents, Henry and Fannie Yoder, had ten children, including two sets of twins: Alvin, then a set of twins; Eli (me) and Levi, Perry, Mahlon, another set of twins; Lester and Esther, Clara, Melvin, and Wilma. There were seven boys and three girls. My brother Levi and I were named according to the Amish tradition of rhyming names for twins. Life unfolded for us on a farm during the 1980s and '90s.

Our farm had a unique layout. The white-sided house, with a black metal roof and curtains stood beside the road—unusual given that most Amish farms had long driveways and were set a distance from the traveled road. Just twenty-five feet off the highway, the house was bordered by a winding driveway that circled it. At the rear of the house was an attached washhouse and a wash-line for drying clothes. Opposite the driveway were all the barns and various outbuildings, which mostly conformed to the Amish tradition of being painted red. Among these was a large barn with an upstairs hayloft with trolleys for loading hay. In total, we had eight other outbuildings, each with a specific purpose. These included spaces for cattle and horses, a place for chickens, an area for hogs, and even a dedicated rabbit building for my twin brother and me. We also had a separate buggy building, a granary equipped with a diesel engine just for grain grinding, and several scattered outbuildings covering a two-acre section of our property.

The driveway extended into the fields and farther into the woods. There were lots of fences to protect the horses and livestock. Beyond this were fields covering approximately ninety acres.

The upstairs of our old farmhouse had three rooms that my siblings and I shared. My twin brother and I, along with my oldest and youngest brothers, shared a bed. The sleeping situation was practical, given the limited space. Our house became especially cold during the winter months when temperatures dropped as low as five degrees below zero. The warmth from the wood stove downstairs barely reached the metal floor register in our uninsulated house, so we often shivered in our beds. The closeness of my siblings was the main source of heat in the winter.

Although the room was often cold, there was comfort in the smell of burning coal on the bitter nights. Coal was added to the stove before bedtime to give heat throughout the night. When we awoke, Mom and Dad would replenish the firewood. The aroma of hickory wood and coal remains etched in my memory, and to this day, its smell makes me feel warm.

In the summer, we fitted screens into the windows. During those sultry summer nights, the songs of locusts and cicadas provided music outside our windows, along with the chorus of our chickens, horses, and cows in the field. In the stillness of the Amish country-side, these sounds carried easily through the night.

Each night as I drifted off to sleep, I could hear the rhythmic ticking of the old wind-up clock in our kitchen. My father faithfully wound the clock's spring each morning, ensuring its gears slowly turned over the next twenty-four hours as its hands kept the time. Since we didn't have electricity or batteries, the clock relied on a spring that kept the pendulum swinging and the gears in motion. Its hypnotic rhythm, 'Tick-tock, tick-tock,' filled my ears as I closed my eyes each night. Soon enough, the sound of Mom's broom handle banging on the metal floor register would rouse me from slumber. "Hey, boys, it's time to milk the cows," she would announce. I'd groan silently as I opened my eyes in anticipation of another long workday that often stretched to sixteen hours, especially in the summer.

I hold these memories close to my heart. The Amish way of life has a peaceful charm, often appearing pure, wholesome, and serene on the surface. Yet, beneath this facade lay closely held secrets that shaped my life in ways I could never have foreseen as a child.

2

EARLY MEMORIES

My earliest memories are of my transition from wearing a dress—a tradition for young children in the Amish community—to wearing pants. It may sound like a simple shift, but it was quite a struggle and left a lasting impression on my young mind.

Every young Amish boy and girl wore cotton dresses until two or three. It made changing homemade cloth diapers a tad more manageable. The Old Order Amish avoided the convenience of store-bought disposable diapers. Instead, my mother expertly folded cloth diapers and often layered them two or three times over to capture the flow of urine. Washing and hanging them on the clothesline took a significant portion of her time, especially with several small children in our household.

I was successfully potty trained at the age of two, but extremely stubborn when the time came to transition out of my dress. My mother insisted, "You're potty trained now. You must wear these pants I've made for you." The homemade denim pants had a row of buttons because zippers were deemed too worldly by the Amish church. My mother patiently demonstrated how the buttons worked, but I wanted no part of the awkward buttons—I liked my dress. I hid under furniture in stubborn determination. Anything to cling to the familiar comfort of my dress.

The dress is my earliest and most vivid memory, not because of the transition itself but because of my deep dislike for change. The idea of giving up my beloved dress, the only clothing I had ever known, filled me with dread. But within our Old Order Amish community, personal preferences had no place. Conformance was enforced through strict discipline, which meant spanking. I had no choice but to comply.

The pants, with four buttons on the front and side, introduced me to a new, intricate ritual. One button had to be undone to pee. I eventually mastered this process after a series of lessons. The pants were far more complex than my simple dress, but they represented a step forward—a step into a world defined by tradition, discipline, and adherence to a way of life that was uniquely Amish.

3

CLOTHING

My early years built a strong work ethic in me as I assisted my mother with various household tasks. Many of us boys held roles inside the house, helping with cleaning, cooking, and even sewing clothes—a task I eventually became quite skilled at. I became so good at sewing that my mother often asked me to stay indoors to assist her with sewing and mending clothes.

Mom was the family's seamstress. She was responsible for creating our clothing at home. She purchased fabric in bulk from the worldly fabric store, though there were strict rules that limited our color choices. The colors were usually dark blue, dark green, gray, black, or white—anything brighter was strictly forbidden. The Amish church's ruling ensured the cotton dresses for young boys and girls were virtually identical. As we got older, these regulations extended to pants, jackets, vests, and hats, each with specific specifications and measurements established by the church's ordinance.

The dress code was clear—girls were not permitted to wear denim material because the ordinance said denim was "a boy thing." Their dresses were made from cotton fabric and occasionally permitted to contain a small percentage of polyester. The Amish church cautioned against the use of overly silky, smooth, or stretchy materials. Mom used plain, flat, smooth fabrics for my sisters' dresses. While some Amish communities might have used stretchy material with a higher polyester content, our church saw the need to remain separate from other Amish groups.

School clothing held a special place in our lives. It had to look immaculate and new, which meant that as soon as a piece of clothing displayed the slightest signs of wear or a small hole appeared, it was patched up and downgraded to at-home use. My pair of pants remained with me throughout my teenage years. Mom skillfully opened the seams with a razor blade and adjusted the belt area to accommodate my growth. She also extended the length of the pant legs as I grew taller. When they became too worn in the seat, she simply flipped them around. Yes, the booty was now in the front!

Our family was obviously poor, which resulted in teasing and bullying at school. Our homemade patched leather shoes were far from the perfect store-bought footwear my classmates wore. I remember in third grade when Mom made us purple shirts—a color permitted by the church at the time. I cherished my purple shirts. But at age nine, my world came crashing down. Mom and Dad returned from church one Sunday and declared that the purple shirt was now "too worldly" and had to be thrown away to please God. I was utterly devastated. I had grown attached to the purple shirts and even assisted Mom in sewing some of them. I impressed my mother with how good I had become at sewing straight seams on shirts and pants. You could say I was a bit of a mama's boy.

4

GRANDPARENTS

Family ties ran deep in our Amish community. The relationships with our parents and grandparents shaped our lives in ways that were both comforting and painful. My maternal grandparents played a significant role in my upbringing.

My grandfather on my dad's side, Alvin Yoder, lived within a mile of our house. Despite our proximity, we didn't have a particularly strong relationship with him. He lived a solitary life. My grandmother had left the Amish years prior. I didn't meet her until I was much older, but our meeting had a profound impact on my life. My mom's parents, Levi and Mable Beechy, lived about two and a half miles away. It's with my maternal grandfather that my story takes a complicated turn. To be honest—I hated my grandfather.

As the leading bishop in the community, my mom's dad was a man of unbending strictness. When I was young, I just thought he was evil and mean. His discipline was swift and harsh. If he caught us doing anything that deviated from Amish rules and regulations, he snatched us up and administered on-the-spot whippings. I remember times when he gripped my ear so hard that I thought it might come off my head. I complained to Mom about it, hoping for sympathy, but she always maintained his authority. She responded by saying, "If he had to do that, it means you were being bad," and then she spanked me again. Eventually, I stopped confiding in Mom about my clashes with him.

My grandmother was a different story. I liked her because she showed kindness and compassion. When my eyesight began to deteriorate, my family couldn't afford to take me to a worldly eye doctor. Grandma stepped in and insisted on hiring a driver to take me to an eye doctor. She saw me struggle to read the blackboard even after I was moved to the front row at the Amish school. I had frequent headaches, and she understood I needed help when no one else seemed to notice. I loved her for the lengths she went to for me. She was strict on occasion and resorted to spankings if we strayed from the rules, but her willingness to get me glasses from the worldly eye doctor earned my respect.

Amish regulations extended even to eyeglasses. I was required to get plain frames without any colorful decorations. The lenses had to be round—like Harry Potter-style—with no added extras or oval shapes permitted.

My grandparents often needed assistance, and my parents would send me to their house to help free of charge. It was the Amish way —grandparents received help from their grandchildren on the farm when needed. It was common to hear Mom and Dad say on a Saturday morning, "Eli, you need to hitch up the horse and buggy, and spend the day helping Grandma and Grandpa." I approached these visits with fear. I knew they required me to walk a straight and narrow line free from missteps, so Mom and Dad received a favorable report, and I avoided a dreaded spanking upon my return.

5

INCOME SOURCES

Our livelihood in the Amish community revolved around one central income source: milk.

Once Mom's broom handle rattled the upstairs heat register to wake us up each morning, there was no room for tardiness. Dad enforced punctuality with a swift walloping if we didn't appear within five minutes of being summoned. We were expected to be up by 4:30 a.m., and by 5:00 a.m., our cows needed to be securely positioned in their stalls, ready for milking. If we failed to have them in place by five o'clock, Dad demanded an explanation and followed up with a walloping.

Our cows were more than just livestock; they were our livelihood. They were trained to respond to the call of their names. We concocted a mixture of grain and molasses to entice them. It was a sweet temptation that always coaxed them to submission, regardless of any discomfort or reluctance. Once they arrived, we slipped a slider around their necks so they remained unmovable. Our milking station consisted of small stools covered with deer hide for comfort.

We would sit barefooted. On occasion, a misstep by a cow led to some pain-filled screaming.

Milking started by squeezing and pulling two teats, alternating between one and the other. The warm milk flowed into a clean stainless-steel bucket. When one side finished, I switched to the two teats on the other side. Afterward, I carried the milk to a carefully cleaned milkhouse with several ten-gallon stainless steel milk cans. A stainless-steel strainer with a thick pad, like a coffee filter, lined the strainer to capture any stray dirt, grime, dust, or chunks that may have found their way into the milk during the milking process.

Once the ten-gallon can was filled, we placed it in the milk tank. The tank contained cold water that was pumped by a five-horse-power gasoline motor the previous night. The chilled water cooled the milk. Several ten-gallon cans were placed within the tank to await the worldly English milkman's arrival around nine o'clock. He collected the milk and transported it to the cheese factory, leaving us with a couple of gallons for our personal use.

We lived without electricity or refrigeration and relied on the freshness of the morning's milk. This milk was unadulterated, unpasteurized, and unhomogenized—it was pure, warm, fresh cow's milk. While some might find it unappealing, it was all we knew. I grew up savoring the flavor of this milk, especially when poured into my homemade grape nut cereal. Sometimes, I enjoyed the simple pleasure of turning a teat while milking and squirting a bit of warm milk into my mouth.

Each morning and evening, I was assigned two cows to milk. One of them was an elderly cow—a respectable eleven years old. She always yielded a five-gallon bucket of milk in the morning and another at the evening milking.

Our Amish rules didn't exempt us from the worldly regulations regarding the handling of milk. Our milk sales to non-Amish customers and the local cheese factory periodically prompted inspections from the health department. As a result, Dad made sure we carefully cleaned every nook and cranny of the milkhouse. To meet health department standards, we even installed smooth white boards on the walls to prevent dust and dirt accumulation. Our Amish community viewed exposure to germs as essential for building a healthy immune system, but we understood that such practices were necessary to avoid offending the sensitivities of the worldly English.

The goats, unlike our beloved cows, were a different story. They carried a distinct, somewhat unpleasant odor that lingered. Milking goats was much more difficult than milking cows. The milk goats produced had a gamey flavor, one that I didn't particularly like, but it served its purpose. Mom often used goat milk to make cottage cheese and other homemade dairy products. Although some of my brothers preferred goat milk with their homemade grape nuts, I could never quite acquire a taste for it.

We followed religious guidelines that prohibited the consumption of certain animals. We did not eat the meat of split-hooved animals such as goats. Instead, we opted to sell them to those who appreciated their unique and special flavor.

6

WORKING WITH MOM

Mom was quite the culinary wizard. She often created a wide array of sweets and treats to sell. She baked pies like pecan, strawberry, and rhubarb, and her shoofly pie was a local favorite. I had my own special task in the kitchen—making bread. The smell of freshly baked bread was something I cherished, and the main reason I was always willing to help Mom around the house.

I wanted to show Mom that I could make homemade maple cluster candies. I loved the maple filling inside them and couldn't resist sneaking a taste when Mom's eyes were elsewhere. I prepared plenty of these candies, mixing up vanilla clusters, maple clusters, and different flavored fillings. First, I'd lay down a bit of chocolate and let it firm up. Then, I'd spoon the filling on top and let it set. Later, I'd pour more melted chocolate from the stove over the top. When it all hardened, we had maple clusters—they looked like solid chunks of chocolate, but hidden inside were delightful maple, vanilla, or strawberry fillings, depending on Mom's creative whim that day. We'd set up shop in front of our farm along the highway with a sign that read "Bake Sale," and folks passing by couldn't resist stopping.

Mom was my kitchen mentor. She taught me various recipes and shared her culinary secrets. I have fond memories of soups bubbling away on our old wood stove. One of them was a German soup called Rivela. Its aroma would always draw me in. I eagerly volunteered to stir the soup and carefully add the ingredients. I don't remember all the details; I do remember those moments when Mom trusted me with the task. My mother's trust and confidence meant a lot to me.

Since Mom knew I had a passion for helping in the kitchen, she often invited me to assist with cake and pie baking, along with soup and bread making. I mixed the bread dough by hand, just the way Mom showed me. I took my role as a dedicated momma's boy seriously. I stayed right there in the kitchen while my older and twin brothers worked alongside Dad. I became quite the young Amish chef.

Our kitchen was a special place, and I learned a lot from Mom. I still recall those shiny hardwood floors. They were so immaculate that if I ever dropped something, I'd simply pick it up and put it right back in the bowl. We weren't obsessed with germs; we were used to being exposed to all sorts of things. Looking back now as a former Amish, it's quite amusing how I'd casually pluck something off the floor and gobble it up.

The memories of those moments in the kitchen, creating all sorts of delicious treats with Mom, remain incredibly special to me. They are cherished treasures that I hold dear.

7

DAD EARNING MONEY

Dad had a knack for crafting various items to sell. He constructed dog houses and decorative roof ornaments known as cupolas, often seen holding weathervanes atop barns. Ironically, the Amish were not allowed to have these items, but the church permitted us to create and sell them to non-Amish folks as a source of income.

He also specialized in crafting log furniture, as well as beds, bed frames, and dresser drawers. Dad would put up a sign and people passing by stopped to purchase his handiwork. Sometimes, they'd even inquire about custom-made furniture for their homes. Dad was always open to trying new ideas. He was quite resourceful and very talented.

Miniature barns were another sought-after item in our community. Dad assisted other Amish men to make these mini barns in various sizes. They were popular because the Amish crafted them from their own wood using their own sawmills to cut the boards. It meant they didn't have significant material expenses. Their only costs were for items like windows and screws purchased from stores, which allowed them to build a mini barn for a couple of hundred dollars and sell it for a substantial profit.

For many years, my dad worked alongside other Amish men and earned an hourly wage of just five dollars. Despite the money Dad earned from these various endeavors, we were considered the poorest family in our entire community. The church and other families often lent us a helping hand whenever they could.

Dad also took on construction work to make ends meet. As my brothers and I got older, we helped him with construction projects away from home. These moments led to some interesting experiences.

My family struggled economically despite my father's talent, physical strength, and work ethic. Dad faced numerous challenges in his life, stemming from a troubled childhood where he witnessed his mom leaving the Amish community due to abuse and neglect. This had a tremendous impact on him, and ultimately, he turned to alcohol for relief. My dad was a great guy when he was sober, but when he was drinking, his behavior was hard to predict. Sometimes he was happy and fun-loving, and willing to engage in adventurous mischief. But more often, he was brooding, angry and abusive. My father's alcohol addiction laid a heavy burden on my family both economically and emotionally; it was a destabilizing and disruptive force. He was like two different people; one I loved and the other I feared. Sadly, my earliest memories of him are filled with fear, as he was often physically abusive to my mom and me and my siblings. My dad's alcoholism touched every area of my family's life and was destined to have a profound impact on me personally.

8

SCHOOL DAYS

By the time I was seven years old, I was eager to start school because my older brother used to talk about his school experiences, and it sounded exciting. I was also eager to escape the turmoil and abuse caused by my dad's addiction. I vividly recall the unique aroma of the wood-burning stove in our one-room schoolhouse. I loved the scent of the smoke that lingered in the air and the radiating warmth and crackling fire on the cold days.

Our school served three or four different Amish churches. Despite having separate church services at various homes, our school was a central place for education. This allowed me to interact and play with kids from other church districts who I wouldn't typically see.

Kindergarten didn't exist in our Old Order Amish community, so I started with first grade and went up to eighth grade. An eighth-grade education was all that was required for our simple way of life. There was no need for higher education for our farming and construction work.

I was excited to attend school because it provided an opportunity to socialize with kids from church and learn English. We spoke Pennsylvania Dutch at home, but we had to learn to speak and write in English starting in second grade. It was an important skill as we progressed through school. English was a bit challenging for me initially, but I excelled in spelling. I had a photographic memory. Once I saw a word, I could remember all its letters, and I took pride in my spelling abilities. We learned the basics of English spelling and some history, although not in detail. We didn't need extensive knowledge of history. Our Amish lifestyle revolved around living and working off the land.

Math was a different story. I struggled with math throughout my time in the Amish school. Our math education was limited to basic operations like addition, subtraction, multiplication, division, and some fractions. We didn't cover advanced math concepts like algebra, geometry, or calculus. In fact, when I was in Amish school, I never even heard of algebra, geometry, or calculus.

Fridays were dedicated to learning formal German, which differed from Pennsylvania Dutch. To become an Amish preacher, you needed to speak formal German during church services, so learning the language was required.

Our teachers were mostly young women, many of them were recent eighth-grade graduates. They were considered qualified to teach right after completing eighth grade. Most were knowledgeable in subjects they excelled in, but some struggled with subjects they weren't strong in, like math. They would often ask smarter students to help others who were struggling.

I had four different teachers throughout my eight years in the Amish school. The teachers varied in age, some as young as fifteen years old. While there were some downsides to having such young teachers, they were knowledgeable and did a good job teaching for the most part.

The role of the school board was to ensure we had access to educational materials from the State of Ohio. The state granted our community a religious exemption so we could have our own private school. They provided us with textbooks for subjects like arithmetic, English (reading, writing, and spelling), geography, and history.

The school board also had authority over school rules and discipline. Teachers could spank and discipline students without parental consent. If we were disciplined at school, we'd most likely get another spanking at home when our parents found out.

Any baptized church member who was eighteen years old and committed to following Amish rules for life could serve on the school board. Every New Year's Day, church members voted for school board candidates, and my oldest brother earned their trust and became the leader of the school board. He handled the school's finances and even had a safe in his house with the school's money. Once the community trusts someone, they're often nominated as the board's chairman or leader.

9

THE ENGLISH

Children were discouraged from interacting with people from the outside world. Outsiders were referred to as "worldly" or "English" people. We were cautioned not to speak to outsiders when they came to buy crafts from my dad or food from my mom. We were told not to start conversations and were required to get a parent when interacting with outsiders. It was an attempt to prevent us from hearing things that might challenge our Amish way of life.

We didn't speak English when we were young, but the worldly music played in their vehicles was considered inappropriate for our ears. Instrumental music was not part of our Amish life, not even in church or school. We were closely monitored to ensure we didn't engage in any worldly activities that might lead us astray.

As we grew older and became more fluent in English, we started interacting with outsiders more often. The more we worked with Dad on construction projects for non-Amish clients, the more we left the safety of our farm. Over time, I developed a fascination with the English way of life and began to admire it.

I was particularly intrigued by certain aspects of their lifestyle, like driving cars and smoking cigarettes. When English people came to our farm to do business, I observed them smoking cigarettes and chewing tobacco. This piqued my curiosity, and I wanted to experience it for myself. On my way to school, I collected discarded cigarette butts that the English people had thrown out of their vehicles. Back home, I lit the cigarette butts with matches. I didn't know how to smoke them; I just smelled the smoke. Even though I didn't fully understand their customs, it felt somewhat thrilling to be more like the English.

We were raised to believe that we stood above the English people, similar to how some Jews might perceive Gentiles. English individuals were considered condemned simply for being born into worldly ways and lost and beyond redemption. We didn't consider the English as lost souls in need of salvation, as some Christians might view unbelievers. We saw no prospect for their redemption. In our Amish community, we firmly held the conviction that we were chosen by God as a special and elect group, while the English served as a source of livelihood. The English lifestyle was consistently presented as something to be avoided at all costs. It served as a symbol of a life destined for eternal damnation and suffering in Hell.

In hindsight, I find the arrogance, pride, and manipulation of these views deeply troubling. However, it's important to highlight that not all Amish communities share these views.

10

DEPRESSION AND ABUSE

My childhood was marked by my father's struggle with alcoholism and the Amish community's response to his actions.

My father's alcohol consumption was strictly prohibited by the Amish church, and the consequences of violating the rules were quite severe. He was frequently shunned by the community, which meant he was cut off from most aspects of Amish life. This extended to our family home. Because he couldn't take anything from another baptized member, including my mother, he was required to make his own food and eat separately in a corner of our kitchen. His separation and isolation were a constant reminder of his struggles and the results they produced. It heaped shame upon his head and, to a larger extent, our whole family.

In our church, my father's status was made very clear. He was separated from the rest of the congregation and made to sit in the "shame corner," a bench reserved for those who were shunned. After each service, the shunned individuals would go upstairs to meet with the preachers. During these meetings, the rules would be discussed, and the church elders would determine whether my father, along with any other rule offenders, would be considered for release from shunning. The forgiveness process ultimately resulted in a vote by the entire church.

Despite his shunning, my father's alcohol addiction persisted. He obtained alcohol when he was with English drivers. Sometimes, he went to gas stations by himself, and other times, the driver purchased alcohol on his behalf. My father was a very sociable and friendly person, and his outgoing demeanor attracted many worldly friends who had no qualms about buying alcohol for him. Occasionally, they even brought alcohol to our Amish farm. They meant no harm and desired to be helpful and friendly, but they had no idea what they were enabling.

I saw my father hide beer in our barn. He placed it in the backside of the haymow where he covered it with hay bales thinking no one would find it. Sometimes, he had as many as ten cases of beer stashed there. He went to such great lengths to conceal his behavior from the church that he would drink his beer warm to avoid being caught.

I witnessed Dad buy beer several times while helping him with construction work. He harnessed the horse to the buggy and drove it to the Mount Victory Ohio Drive-Thru. As he tied off the horse by the hitching rack or utility pole, onlookers often found it amusing that an Amish man was buying beer in such a typical manner. I can't deny the reality of seeing my dad purchase alcohol with my own eyes.

When Dad was shunned for repeatedly breaking the rules, he often unleashed his frustration and anger on us children, subjecting us to physical abuse. There were also instances when he violently assaulted my mother. I recall those terrifying moments when I cowered under furniture, fearing for my life, as I watched my mother endure unimaginable torment. I'll never forget one particularly harrowing incident where he wrapped his jacket around her throat, tied a knot, and pulled it tight, causing her face to turn blue. I lay there in terror, convinced that she might not survive, and waited anxiously until she regained consciousness.

In our quest for safety, my mom, my siblings, and I became nomads. We constantly sought refuge in the homes of my aunts and uncles. We knew Dad's unpredictable temper could erupt at any moment when he drank, and we had to stay away to protect ourselves. Sometimes, other compassionate members of the Amish community would step in to assist us with household chores during these times. They understood the importance of keeping us safe until Dad's anger subsided.

Despite the turmoil at home, the Amish community didn't remain idle. The Amish men, including elders and bishops, often visited our home to reason with my father and attempt to bring peace to our family. But when Dad was intoxicated, their efforts were futile, and he chased them off. Sometimes he even brandished a rifle to ensure they left our property.

I distinctly remember one incident when my mother decided to take my siblings and me to our aunt and uncle's house in a desperate attempt to escape my father's violent outburst. As I peered out the window in terror, I saw my drunk father chasing an Amish bishop down the highway. In an intoxicated rage, he kicked and punched him. The bishop clutched his hat in his hand while he dodged the blows and tried desperately to escape harm.

My father's violent tendencies posed a constant threat to our family and challenged the Amish community. Despite my mother's dedication to our safety, we lived in perpetual fear of my father's unpredictable actions.

The church had strict rules against reporting crimes to law enforcement, which left my mother with limited options. Any attempt to involve outside authorities would have resulted in her being shunned by the church community, a fate she was eager to avoid. She chose to confide in her father, the bishop of our Amish church. When my mother approached him with the details of my father's abusive behavior, the response from the church was to extend my father's shunning period. This was seen as a form of punishment, but it did not involve seeking help from secular authorities or engaging with outsiders.

At times, my father was alone on the farm for several weeks while my mother and siblings stayed away to ensure our safety. The church used this time to intervene by trying to send him to an Amish reform facility. They believed my father's soul was in peril and that without reform, he would face eternal damnation. Under this pressure, my father sometimes relented and agreed to cease drinking alcohol and get clean. But these periods of apparent change were usually short-lived. After a few weeks or months, my father inevitably relapsed into alcohol abuse, and the cycle of physical abuse against us and my mother resumed.

For the most part, my siblings and I maintained amicable relationships with each other until our teenage years. When my father's condition deteriorated further, my oldest brother, Alvin, and I fell into disagreement and conflict. In my father's absence as a stable figure in the household, my older brother assumed a leadership role by necessity. His newfound authority led to disagreements and arguments between us. Despite these occasional conflicts, our sibling bonds remained strong. It was our father who instilled the greatest fear in us as we witnessed him commit acts that left us concerned for our mother's and our own safety.

My father once brought a sledgehammer into the house after a heated argument with my mother. She had locked herself in the bedroom to find refuge, but it did not deter my father. He used the sledgehammer to forcibly break down the bedroom door and sent the doorknob flying. Once the door was reduced to splinters, he subjected my mother to further physical abuse.

While my father typically used objects like a broom handle or his fists to inflict harm on my mother, his most brutal attacks involved furniture or chairs. My mother still bears visible scars from these beatings.

Both the church and my mother's sisters were aware of the abuse she endured at the hands of my father. The bruises on her body were an undeniable reminder of the violence within our home. Despite my father's repeated shunning, his behavior continued to escalate behind closed doors.

My father never faced any legal repercussions for the severe physical abuse he inflicted on our family. The Amish church's belief in forgiveness and redemption meant that any crimes committed by its members, no matter how severe, were ultimately considered forgivable. When the church chose to shun an individual as punishment, the expectation was that they would eventually reform their behavior and be welcomed back into the community. However, my father's repetitive cycle of violence and eventual forgiveness only perpetuated the ongoing abuse inflicted upon us.

My father's repeated relapses demonstrated that this system was ineffective in both addressing the root causes of his actions and providing adequate protection for his victims. The fact that he knew he would eventually be forgiven created a dangerous cycle of abuse, where he would temporarily repent of his behavior to gain reinstatement within the community, only to revert to his abusive ways once forgiveness was granted. This left my family vulnerable to ongoing abuse and trauma. It was a perpetual cycle that would eventually meet a tragic ending.

11

REFORM HOUSE

O ur community had our version of a Reform House, which we called the Amish Counseling Facility. This was a home where Amish bishops and elders rehabilitated people who were troubled, including young teenagers who wanted to leave the Amish. Troubled individuals were sent there to get "fixed." It's not a licensed facility staffed with certified counselors. It's just an Amish home with maybe a dozen bedrooms. The residents helped with farm work while undergoing various counseling sessions. They were guided towards thinking in the Amish way and submitting to the Amish church, its rules, and its leadership. They employed methods that some might consider brainwashing or psychological manipulation, and even utilized drugs and fear tactics to achieve their desired end.

They wanted my dad to go there, but he didn't tolerate it for very long. He simply didn't put up with it. They sent other Amish church members who had been baptized and later had thoughts of leaving the Amish. Sometimes they used licensed English doctors to obtain

Xanax to treat depression and other medications that are illegal to dispense. Some doctors trusted Amish leadership enough to prescribe Adderall and other drugs, which the Amish used to medicate and coerce individuals into conforming to the Amish church and subsequent way of life.

After leaving the Amish, I tried to raise awareness and expose some of those illegal facilities. Not only are they unauthorized, but they lack certification, proper training, and pose a significant danger. Essentially, their purpose is to reprogram individuals who disagree with their theology or rules. In my opinion, these reform houses should be shut down. I remember thinking about leaving as a teenager and discussing it with outsiders; I wouldn't dare discuss my concerns with another Amish person. If anyone showed interest in the outside worldly life, they instantly referred them to that place so they could be medicated and coerced into surrender.

12

WORK AT HOME

We received our daily assignments and rules during breakfast. I would hear phrases like "You're helping Mom today," or "You're going out to the garden today," or "You're hitching up the horse and assisting the community with a barn raising," or "You're working in the fields today, plowing, discing, and cultivating corn," and so on.

During my preschool years, I mostly worked inside the house or out in the garden. Mom taught me how to pull weeds, harvest vegetables, cut potatoes, and can them.

Our garden was quite extensive. It featured sweet corn, red beets, carrots, cucumbers, and much more. Cucumbers were particularly important because we needed them to make pickles, a staple for Sunday's church meal. We also grew onions, potatoes, cauliflower, broccoli, peas, and asparagus.

Mom was known for her pies. We had a strawberry patch, too. The strawberry rhubarb pie was especially popular, and it never stayed on the table for long.

We canned all these vegetables using a pressure cooker to process and seal the jars. At six years old, I helped Mom by putting the seals on the jars and adding a bit of salt. We went through large bags of salt during the canning season. A pinch of salt was placed on top of the contents of each jar, whether it was beets, green beans, pickles, peas, or even the meat we butchered. We added a little water, sealed the lid with a screw-on ring, and then used the pressure cooker to create a vacuum that sealed the jar. We stored the jars in the basement.

It was typical to have a thousand jars of meat and vegetables in the basement. Each day, Mom selected the vegetables she wanted to prepare for breakfast, lunch, and dinner. The boys were tasked with checking the seals on the jars before every meal. I distinctly remember the sound of "dink-dink." If the seal was broken, the sound was dull, more like a "dunk." If the seal had been broken, there was likely some mold inside. You're probably thinking we threw moldy food away, but you're wrong!

Wasting food was strictly forbidden. Nothing was thrown away, even if it had a bit of mold. Mom would take the mold and mix it in. She firmly believed that mold was beneficial, claiming it was like penicillin for the body and would help build our immune systems. We consumed our fair share of mold, and no one suffered any ill effects. If anyone ever died from botulism, we never knew it. I doubt it ever happened.

Pies were stored in the pantry, and while we didn't have refrigerators or electricity, it didn't matter because they usually disappeared within a day. If a pie did sit for two or three days and developed a slight greenish fuzz, we still ate it. Mold was not a deterrent; it was more like a condiment. I consumed lots of mold during my time in the Amish, which might explain why I didn't get sick very often.

We didn't buy any of our food from stores. Everything we consumed was produced on our farm—homegrown vegetables and meat from our pigs, chickens, and cattle.

When I started first grade, Dad began giving me assignments in the barn and the fields. Later, when I became strong enough to milk a cow, I was considered strong enough to operate my own horse and buggy. I was determined to prove to Mom and Dad that I could milk a cow, and by the age of seven, I accomplished it. I milked two cows every morning at 5:00 and again in the afternoon at 5:00, and my brothers did the same.

After milking cows, my brothers and I often argued on our way to school about who would get to drive the horse. My twin brother, my older brother, and I took turns driving the horse to school.

Slaughtering a cow was a major event, and we always worked together. As early as age five, Mom and Dad required us to assist in the slaughtering process. Every winter, we slaughtered one cow and one hog. We learned how to shoot them, open them up, remove the guts, and cut the meat into specific pieces. Just like everything else, we canned the meat.

By the time I was ten, I knew how to slaughter a cow. After leaving the Amish, I realized that to the outside world, what we did was considered child labor abuse. There are laws that protect children from such work.

Child labor was the norm in our community, and we helped Dad in the fields and with chores from a young age. Our labor was essential to the farm's operation, and it made us physically strong. My siblings and I worked diligently, and our efforts were expected. Despite English laws on child labor, I don't regret those experiences because they instilled a strong work ethic in me, and I still cherish many of those memories.

13

OUR KITCHEN

Our Amish kitchen was incredibly spacious, measuring about 20 x 30 feet. It featured an open layout with a homemade sink without a drain pipe, as we didn't have running water or sewer. At the end of the sink we had a homemade dish rack. While some Amish families used store-bought versions, ours was crafted from wood and had hooks, slots for plates, compartments for glasses, and slots for silverware. It even had a little cup holder. Everything was homemade. Water drained from this rack onto a stainless steel strainer that my dad had built into the wooden sink. From there, it flowed down to a plug in one corner that could be removed, allowing the water to collect in a bucket below. We emptied this bucket outside whenever it got full.

At the end of the sink was a hand pump connected to a hose that reached down to our cistern. Our cistern was essentially a large underground reservoir located beneath the washhouse. Cisterns were used to collect rainwater, and the hand pump would draw that water up through the hose into a stainless steel bucket and bowls. Mom warmed this water to wash dishes.

The same cistern water served another crucial purpose. On Saturday nights, we were treated to baths, a tradition among the Old Order Amish. We used a galvanized, oval-shaped metal tub, and I distinctly remember the smell of the galvanized metal as I lay in it. Mom's homemade soap, crafted from pig fat (lard) was used for washing. The scent of lard brings back memories. While we did use store-bought Crisco oil occasionally, lard was our primary choice for shortening, greasing pans, and frying. It also played a key role in making homemade soap. Mom mixed other ingredients that added a pleasant scent to the soap, but it effectively removed the grime and sweat from our weekly toils on the farm, especially the strenuous task of putting up hay.

Each week, we diligently wiped down the kitchen until everything gleamed. On Saturday mornings, it was our responsibility to help Mom clean the walls, ceiling, and floor, which is why they always appeared shiny and spotless.

Our kitchen, with its bare walls, holds special memories. There were no pictures or decorations except the large clock hanging on one wall. If anything did hang on the walls, it was likely a tool or utensil that Mom used for cooking, like a tomato masher, tomato juicer, or applesauce press. Apart from that, it was just the clock and a calendar—yes, we did use a calendar.

In the center of our spacious kitchen sat a table where as many as twenty-five people could gather comfortably. The table was always covered with a waterproof canvas-style cover, making it easy to clean. We wiped it down after every meal.

The only source of light was from a holder protruding from the windowsill holding a kerosene lamp. We purchased kerosene from the worldly English people who brought bulk tanks for us. Kerosene served as the fuel for our oil lamps. We also used kerosene for a specialized oven designed for baking bread. The kerosene heat was incredibly efficient for this purpose.

Overall, the kitchen was practical and amazingly efficient despite the lack of modern technology.

14

FOOD

We ate together as a family at the table in the mornings and for dinner in the evening. It was essential that we all gathered as a family. We'd bow our heads and silently offer a prayer. The prayer was never spoken aloud because that was considered the practice of worldly people. I didn't know how to pray, so I would simply listen to the rhythmic tick-tock of our old wind-up clock. That was the only sound I heard when it was completely silent. After a few minutes, Dad scuffed his feet on the floor, signaling that the prayer was over. Then, we'd lift our heads and pass one bowl at a time around the table, and everybody would take a scoop of food.

The food at our home was mostly delicious. My mom always prepared food from scratch, and I often tell people that I miss homemade food the most. Many of these dishes had German names I can't remember.

Chicken was a big part of our diet in the Amish community. We raised our own chickens. They laid eggs, and before the next batch of chicks arrived the following year, we butchered them. Chicken was prepared in various ways—fried, grilled, and baked. My mom was particularly skilled at baked chicken dishes.

One of my favorite childhood memories was making Amish peanut butter. When I was young, Amish peanut butter was my absolute favorite. I was allowed to mix four simple ingredients together: a jar of creamy peanut butter, Karo syrup, marshmallow fluff, and hot water. It was a straightforward recipe, and I was always enthusiastic to help. I used my fingers throughout the process, which usually resulted in a sugar buzz before I finished. When Mom made it, the recipe yielded twelve jars, but when I made it, somehow we ended up with only ten jars. The other two jars were in my belly!

Maple clusters were another favorite of mine because I liked anything maple-flavored. But like Amish peanut butter, when I prepared them we ended up with a bit less product.

There were also some dishes I couldn't stand. One of them was Rivela soup, known as *Rivela Suppe* in German. It was a soup that contained chunks of potatoes and pieces of flour. My mom would add flour, sugar, and salt to it. The texture and flavor were nauseating, so I only took a tiny bit to appease my parents. Wasting food was not allowed; we had to eat what was made, but I truly despised that dish.

My mom also made another dish with a German name that resembled sauerkraut but had some additional ingredients that gave it a bitter taste. I could hardly tolerate it.

There were a few more dishes that I didn't enjoy, such as potato, flour, and cracker soup. Mom prepared cracker soup on Saturdays, which was bath night. Saturdays were busy, and Mom had a lot of work to do between cooking and warming up water. Cracker soup was a salty dish made with white crackers, warmed-up milk, and flour. The texture was chunky, and eating it felt like chewing rubber. I couldn't stand it. I dreaded Saturday nights when Mom was busy because she always made that dish. Everything about it made me cringe, from its texture to its smell.

On Sunday mornings, Mom prepared coffee soup. She took chunks of bread, sprinkled brown sugar on it, and poured coffee over it to make the bread soggy. It was an Amish soup we had every Sunday morning because we needed to milk the cows and prepare for church. Mom didn't have much time to prepare an elaborate meal, so we had to eat whatever she made.

Most of the food we had, including pies, cakes, desserts, candies, and chocolates, was incredibly delicious. There were no preservatives in these homemade treats. They were all made from homegrown ingredients, making them much healthier than processed foods in the worldly markets. Perhaps this is why the Amish tend to live to ripe old ages. They are always physically active, working hard, and burning calories. The food they prepare from their own resources is far healthier and lacks the additives found in mainstream food. When I left the Amish and started reading the ingredient lists on packaged foods, it was quite shocking. I couldn't even pronounce some of the words. They put preservatives in everything!

We never dined at a restaurant. The Old Order conservative group of Amish discouraged us from eating at worldly restaurants. When we were traveling with hired drivers, Dad and Mom instructed the driver not to stop at a restaurant. They even discouraged us from fast food places, although there were occasional exceptions. The church preferred that we didn't sit down at a restaurant to eat. I didn't experience dining at a regular restaurant until after I left the Amish.

We never had store-bought cereal, but we often ate homemade cereal known as "grape nuts." My mom had other German names for her homemade cereal, but I can't recall how to pronounce them. Speaking Pennsylvania Dutch was a skill I lost after leaving the Amish; if you don't use it, you lose it. I remember passing the bowl around, and everyone had to eat everything on their plate. The rule was simple: if you didn't finish what was on your plate, you'd get a spanking and no dessert. Dad had a wooden paddle with a custom-made belt, complete with holes that could sting when used on my behind. I knew that not eating everything on my plate, like the sauerkraut I detested, would lead to a spanking.

15

DAILY LIFE

The absence of electricity and television meant we read a lot of books and newspapers. But it didn't take long for me to notice that these reading materials had holes where Mom and Dad had carefully cut out any images of worldly people wearing shorts, showing their legs, or women with their hair uncovered. Such imagery was strictly forbidden and considered a potential source of lust or temptation and was believed to bring a curse upon us. To avoid this, they carefully removed these images from books and newspapers, leaving only the words for us to read. All our reading materials were subject to strict approval, and certain books, especially those related to worldly history or topics like world wars, were strictly forbidden.

In our Amish household, we had no indoor plumbing. This was true even in our church, which was held within our homes. Men went to the barn, while women used the outhouse. The outhouse was separate from the main house and had no flushing toilets. It was simply an open hole. Once the deed was done, it would fall to the ground at the bottom of the hole. Once a year, the contents of the outhouse hole were shoveled out and used as fertilizer in the fields.

Indoor plumbing and running water were luxuries we did not have. We used the water from the pump in the kitchen sink for most purposes. To warm it, we used a wood-burning stove. For bathing, we dumped hot water into a tub and mixed it with cold to achieve a comfortable temperature.

Drinking water came from a well, not the cistern. We had a separate pump located in the washhouse with a five-horsepower motor that was occasionally reduced to two-and-a-half horsepower. These motors were exclusively used for pumping water and filling livestock tanks through underground pipes. When we opened the spigot, water flowed into tanks throughout the barns to ensure the animals were well-hydrated.

We drank water from a clean, stainless-steel bucket that was filled daily and placed in a convenient location. There was only one cup for everyone to use, and its handle had seen its share of dirty hands. We didn't concern ourselves with germs; exposure to such elements was believed to be beneficial for our immune systems. This communal cup was dipped into the bucket by each family member for a drink. The water from the well had a distinctive rusty flavor, which I can taste even today. To me, it was delicious.

When I left the Amish and began drinking purified bottled water from Walmart, I thought it tasted terrible because it lacked the familiar rust flavor. I had always appreciated the well water's unique taste, which I believed to be good for me.

Refrigerators were considered too worldly by the church, so we never owned one. In the summer, we made use of a small icebox to keep the milk cool. Each morning, we'd add a chunk of ice to the box. A daily trip to the Amish icehouse was required to replace the melted chunk. To harvest ice, we ventured onto the frozen ponds of the worldly English people during the winter months, using hand saws to cut the ice into bricks. By age four, I was allowed to help move the saw up and down to cut the ice. The ice bricks were stored in the icehouse and surrounded by foam crumbs and sometimes sawdust to keep them from melting. Despite the sweltering mid-July temperatures, the icehouse was able to maintain the ice with minimal melting. We'd brush away the foam crumb until we reached an intact brick, which we'd take home and place in the icebox alongside items like jam, jelly, butter, milk, and leftover pie. All other foods didn't require refrigeration.

During the winter, refrigeration was unnecessary. We stored perishables in the pantry where the cool temperature was maintained naturally, away from house heating. Our vegetables were canned, as was our meat, using pressure cookers. Whatever Mom opened for a particular day's meal was consumed entirely that day.

The kerosene lamps had glass chimneys, and we'd lift them off to light the wick with a match. Lighters were prohibited, so we had to rely on matches. We'd adjust the wick to a soft glow, and later, a small round plate placed behind the oil lamp on the wall was introduced, covered with aluminum foil to enhance the brightness. The foil covered plate produced a slightly brighter light, and I recall the excitement when this addition was adopted in Amish homes. Some members had reservations and though it was too worldly, but after much discussion and a vote, it was widely accepted.

16

MEDICAL CARE

Most Amish communities today have evolved to allow their members to go to the hospital and even call an ambulance in case of emergencies. But my family followed a tradition rooted in unwavering faith and trust in God. There was a strong belief that when faced with illness or injury, one had to place their faith in God entirely. I experienced this firsthand when I suffered a severe injury in fifth grade. I fell from fifty feet, broke my ribs on the left side, and lost consciousness. I had no idea the extent of my injuries when I regained consciousness the next day. I opened my eyes, surrounded by my family, who believed my fate rested solely in God's hands. They held a gathering in advance of my funeral. Many of my aunts, uncles, and cousins, as well as members of my extended family were present. The consensus was clear: it was a matter of life or death, and my fate was with God alone. They did not mention calling an ambulance or hiring a driver. It was simply, "He either lives or he dies." In the end, I survived.

Under the church's rules, we were allowed to use basic over-the-counter pain medications such as Tylenol, Aleve, and Excedrin. These were the only medicines at our disposal. In the absence of hospital visits, I relied on Tylenol to alleviate the excruciating pain I experienced. My mother extracted juice from aloe vera plants, which she used for various remedies. These remedies were intended for specific illnesses and conditions, but they offered no relief from pain, so I lay there, taking Tylenol to manage the pain. It was an agonizing experience, but it was the only option available to me.

In some cases, members of our community did go to the hospital, but it was rare. My father had some basic medical knowledge, so he played the role of the family dentist. If I had a painful or infected tooth, he would use a pair of pliers to extract it. We were a poor family, and spending money on a dentist was out of the question. While the church didn't explicitly forbid visiting dentists or doctors, my parents simply chose not to spend money on such services.

Upon leaving the Amish community, I quickly realized the stark differences in how the Amish valued human life compared to the wider world. The English place a high value on human life and invest heavily in healthcare, emergency services, and medical professionals. They learn CPR and first aid and make use of safety measures. Paramedics, EMTs, nurses, doctors, and the fire department are trained to save lives, and calling 911 was a common practice. In stark contrast, these services were mostly absent in the Amish community, which reflects a different perspective on the value of human life.

Animals were valuable within the Amish culture, especially horses. They were vital for transportation and labor and were well cared for and cherished within our community, often more so than humans.

Our family, consisting of eight members at the time, was traveling by buggy along a highway when a car struck us from behind. Our buggy shattered into pieces and reduced to splinters. The accident left my mother lying in the middle of the road, as a semi-truck came to a screeching halt just inches from her head. We were all thrown around, bleeding from open gashes and cuts.

Several people in other vehicles had mobile phones and dialed 911. Multiple ambulances arrived on the scene because it was a large Amish family with numerous injuries. But when the EMS personnel arrived, they were met with the shock of their lives. My parents firmly declined their offer to transport us to the hospital, citing a lack of funds. They believed we would heal at home and placed our lives entirely in God's hands. They declared, "If we die, we die; if we live, we live."

The EMS personnel were shocked; their expressions revealed their concern. They saw us poor children with blood running down our faces, arms, and legs, and were astonished that my parents would refuse to allow us to go to the hospital. They were left with no choice but to prepare the paperwork for my parents to sign that would absolve them of any responsibility. It was a startling and eye-opening experience for everyone involved.

17

HOLIDAYS AND CELEBRATIONS

W e didn't observe traditional birthdays or holidays in the Amish community. Birthdays were just another day of hard work, absent of cakes, candles, or presents. We did have a unique tradition for birthdays in our Amish home. On my birthday, my siblings and parents would playfully push me under the table for about five to ten minutes. They'd all share in laughter and wish me a "Happy birthday." This was our unconventional way of celebrating birthdays, then it was back to work as usual. Don't try to find any special meaning behind this tradition; I'm fairly certain there is none.

As baptized members of the church, our parents followed certain fasting practices during religious holidays. On holidays like Easter, a time of fasting was observed. Parents were not allowed to eat, but children could snack while our parents abstained from food.

There was also a celebration known as "Old Christmas" held on January 6th. This date was believed to be the actual birthdate of

Jesus. During Old Christmas, my parents would fast while my siblings and I were permitted to snack and engage in games.

In contrast to these fasting holidays, the Amish community did celebrate a more conventional Christmas on December 25th. We gathered with family, prepared meals, made candy, and enjoyed a grand feast together. No gifts were exchanged, no Christmas trees were erected with decorations and lights, and there was definitely no mention of Santa Claus. These English traditions are considered pagan by the Amish community. What I do remember from these celebrations is the delicious aroma of chicken cooking for Christmas dinner. Amish recipes for chicken are incredibly appetizing, and it was always a highlight of these feasts. The food at these gatherings was delicious; I can taste it in my memories.

One of the most popular and common Amish feasts in my community was called a "haystack." It involved piling about fifty different food items onto a large Amish plate, twice the size of a regular Styrofoam plate. The food was stacked up to a foot high. We'd layer lettuce, carrots, chopped vegetables, cheese, mashed potatoes, gravy, crushed chips from the worldly store, and numerous other ingredients. You could include meat, chicken, salads, and a variety of other dishes. What made haystacks so unique was that you didn't reach to serve yourself from the various bowls of food. Instead, bowls of food were passed around the table from person to person, and you took a little of each item. By the time it made its way around, it looked like a literal haystack. It was a classic Amish feast, and I still enjoy making it today and introducing my non-Amish family to some of the dishes we used to prepare. It's always a hit, and the combination of flavors is simply delicious.

One personal favorite of mine when making haystacks was the runny melted cheese that we poured over the top that soaked into all the ingredients. It added a delightful touch to an already delicious meal.

18

AMISH CHURCH

A ttending Amish church services as a child was a mix of excitement and anxiety. It was a day when I could play with other kids, but it was also a time when my father often faced shunning or confrontation from the church elders.

On Sundays, our church services were held in individual homes, as the Old Order Amish do not have dedicated church buildings. Services rotated between families, and the benches were transported on wooden wagons. Every family had a turn to host the church service. The women sat in rows in the kitchen while the men occupied the living room. The teenagers, ranging from twelve to seventeen, sat at the back, and unmarried individuals sat behind the teenagers in the youth group.

The church service itself included singing hymns from German songbooks. We sang without the accompaniment of musical instruments. Amish children learn to sing in harmony from an early age through daily singing in Amish schools. By the time they're baptized, they have memorized hundreds of German hymns, which they sing without the need for a book. A leader starts the song, and the congregation follows in perfect harmony, creating a beautiful and distinctive sound.

The preachers deliver their sermons from memory without opening a Bible. The Amish use the 1522 Martin Luther German Bible exclusively. They claim it to be the only true Word of God.

During the church service, a snack of homemade church cookies, known as "gma cookies" (gma meaning *church* in German), was passed around for the children. A meal of peanut butter, marshmallow cream, and karo syrup was served on homemade bread immediately after service with cheese spread, pickles, and red beets. Tea or coffee was also served to complete a traditional Sunday meal for the congregation.

The structure of Amish church districts typically included twenty to forty families, and when a district grew too large, it split into two or more districts. Each district has three preachers and one bishop, chosen through a process of nomination and casting of lots.

It's important to note that Amish church services are not open to outsiders; non-Amish individuals are not welcome to attend. The service is conducted entirely in German, and only those who follow Amish rules and have been accepted into the church are allowed to participate.

One unique aspect of Amish church services is the intense focus on the Amish way of life. The Amish do not emphasize the concept of being *born again* like many Christian denominations. They believe that living as an Amish person and adhering to their rules and traditions represents being born again. This perspective is reinforced through preaching and teaching.

Fear is a common tactic used to control and discourage members from leaving the Amish community. Preachers often emphasize the idea that only the Amish are chosen by God and those who leave will face eternal damnation. This fear-based approach is used to keep young members from straying from the Amish way of life, and it's highly effective.

Sermons often included stories about people who left the Amish and suffered some horrible fate that was directly attributed to their leaving. I recall one story about a young man who left and was tragically killed in a car accident a short time later. The preacher delivered this story with deep emotion and tears. He cried over the heartbreaking loss of this young man and his certain damnation. The implied message was that God would kill anyone who left the Amish. This story had a significant impact on me.

Sundays are a day of rest and leisure for the Amish. We were permitted to milk the cows and tend to the animals, but other work was strictly prohibited, and we could not spend any money. It was a day when Amish children looked forward to playing games in the barn or at home. It was a welcome break from the daily chores and routines of Amish life.

19

DECEIVED

On the non-church Sundays, Mom and Dad gathered us at home and said, "It's time to read a few verses from the German Bible." Those moments usually lasted about two or three minutes, and I recited the verses quickly.

My parents lacked the knowledge to interpret the Bible or provide explanations for what I read. Their guidance was simply, "God is pleased if you read it." We were never offered any interpretations or insights into its meaning. If we wanted a deeper understanding, we were told to consult the elders and the bishop. Questioning the Bible's meaning or seeking alternative explanations was discouraged; it was considered prideful to attempt a personal interpretation.

I was raised to believe that excessive Bible reading could lead to deception by the Devil and draw us away from our cherished traditions. Our articles of faith held more authority than the Bible itself. I distinctly remember thinking, 'Our articles of faith, authored by Jakob Ammann, the founder of the Amish, make us special.' This idea was fueled by the belief that our rules and regulations surpassed those of other Amish communities and signified that we were a chosen group in the eyes of God.

It was ingrained in us at an early age that we were even more exceptional than the remnant Jews of ancient Israel. My mother often spoke about the 144,000 mentioned in the Book of Revelation and asserted that we were part of that select group. But when our Amish population exceeded 144,000, the narrative had to be adjusted. My mother once remarked, "Well, we used to think that Jesus would return and take us home before our numbers exceeded 144,000." In hindsight, this should have been a clear indicator that this belief was not accurate.

We took immense pride in our perceived uniqueness, our meticulous adherence to rules, our virtuous deeds, and our self-righteous way of life. The concept of salvation through Jesus was never part of our upbringing. Instead, we were taught that those in the English community who professed to be saved were displaying arrogance and pride because one could not be certain of their salvation. I recall overhearing conversations with English people who stopped to buy baked goods. While I sat there, selling my mom's baked goods, they would inquire, "You're Christians, being Amish, right?"

Our condescending yet pleasant response was always, "Oh yes, indeed."

They would continue, "So you must understand that you can be saved. Praise God. We're saved, too. I'm so thankful that Jesus died for our sins."

Despite their good intentions, they assumed we shared their understanding, but that was far from the truth. I simply shook my head and thought, 'No, you've been misled.' They had no inkling that my faith and hope for Heaven were firmly rooted in the rules and regulations of the Amish church. I was indoctrinated to believe that anyone claiming salvation through the finished work of the cross was exhibiting excessive pride, and I was cautioned to distance myself from such "dangerous" thinking.

It would take many years for me to cast off these misconceptions and embrace genuine truth—that Jesus is indeed the way, the truth, and the life, and that no one comes to the Father except through Him.

PART 2

COMING OF AGE

20

NEW RESPONSIBILITIES

Coming of age as an Amish youth brings a lot of responsibility. When you enter your teenage years, you're no longer seen as a child; you're expected to work like a man. This is a stark contrast to the English world, where teenagers often face feelings of boredom, depression, and perceived uselessness.

In the Amish community, I had to learn how to harness a horse, plow fields, operate a disc, shuck corn and cut corn, plant crops, and participate in crop harvesting—all of these tasks were expected of me. Falling short in any of these areas or being slow led to ridicule, mockery, and even bullying. Amish men were judged based on their performance of these basic tasks. These skills were deemed essential to the Old Order Amish way of life.

I struggled to meet many of these expectations. I was a slow learner and often felt like an underachiever, especially compared to my twin brother who excelled and learned quickly. My sense of inadequacy led to a growing desire to leave the Amish community as early as age twelve. But I wasn't sure how to make my escape. I worried that if I tried, I might fail, and my doubts about following through held me back. I was determined to find a way out because I was deeply unhappy, and, in truth, I was battling what I now recognize as severe depression.

21

HORSE TRAINING

Training horses for our English neighbors was a thrilling experience that my brothers and I loved. It also provided some much-needed income for personal spending. Mounting an unbroken horse and soaring through the air rodeo-style was an adrenaline rush like nothing else. Even though we got thrown off and suffered some bruises and probably a few untreated broken bones along the way, we couldn't get enough of it. We felt like tough rebels, capable of taming horses that had never been ridden before. Riding them, breaking them in, and feeling the power beneath us was a thrill we couldn't resist.

But, as with just about everything else we enjoyed, the Amish church took issue with our horse-training ventures. We were not allowed to ride astride, whether it was bareback or with a saddle. When we were spotted riding this way, someone would complain. It happened enough that it led to a church decision that put an end to our horse training days. The church considered us prideful for imitating worldly Western riding. We were devastated by the church's decision, but my brothers and I didn't give up easily—we found another way.

We came up with a plan to continue riding and breaking horses. We told our English customers that we would work the horses in the fields between the wood lots. Woods surrounded a field with a road leading through the woods to the open clearing. We started breaking horses there, having just as much fun as before while keeping it hidden from the church. Even Dad hadn't known about it for a long time.

When Dad eventually discovered our secret activities, he didn't seem too concerned, but he told us we were risking getting him into more trouble. We continued breaking horses because it was too enjoyable to give up. We didn't care about the potential consequences.

We also managed to keep some of the money we earned hidden from our parents, which we used to buy things like throwaway cameras. I used the cameras to photograph the farm and capture moments and memories. But when my Mom came across a camera hidden in my sock drawer, she burned it with all my photos. It was a heartbreaking loss of some incredible memories that I wish I could have preserved.

Breaking horses was fun, in large part because it was a forbidden activity. We felt satisfaction from doing it without anyone knowing. But eventually, the risk it posed to my father outweighed the benefits. We had a wonderful time for a few months, but our careers as rodeo cowboys came to an end a few months after it began, and our interests moved elsewhere.

22

THE PALLET SHOP

One morning at the breakfast table, my dad asked my twin brother and me if we were willing to work at the pallet shop. It was owned by worldly English people. My brother and I were about sixteen years old at the time, an age when we could be employed for basic labor. The pallet shop specialized in building pallets used by various businesses to transport products and equipment. Pallets keep items off the ground and provide a convenient surface for forklifts to raise and move them. Pallets may seem crude and void of fancy technology, but they fulfill an important function in daily life. Ironically, they are still a part of my everyday life.

The financial struggles my family faced were a constant challenge. One day Dad said to my brother and me, "We just need to send two of you boys down there. I've talked to the owner, and we can earn some money. He will pay by the hour, and you can bring the money home." In the Amish community, individuals aren't allowed to have their own money until they are twenty-one years old. We understood that whatever money we earned, we'd have to hand over to Mom and Dad.

I had worked with English people before and genuinely enjoyed being around them. Conversations with them made me feel happy. They smelled good, always seemed to be smiling, and radiated warmth. There was no sense of rejection or ridicule. If we stumbled or struggled with something, they'd say, "It's okay. We'll teach you." They'd patiently help us until we became proficient in a new task. It was a huge difference from the environment at home, where I didn't receive that kind of support.

Our jobs were simple. We did a lot of stacking and sorting of finished pallets; they were always piled twenty to a stack. The atmosphere was charged with energy and excitement. The machinery made lots of noise and smoke. The bandsaws produced a distinctive burned smell when the wood got hot; the odor filled the whole shop and the surrounding area. The smell of the gasoline and chainsaw exhaust was foreign to us, but I thought it smelled good.

There was a radio playing worldly music, which intrigued me. The Amish scorned musical instruments, but worldly music had many instruments and it was appealing to my ears. Here, I could listen to tunes that I found fascinating—the music made me feel good.

During my time at the pallet shop, I was introduced to worldly foods like hamburgers, french fries, Wendy's, and other foods we could never taste in our Amish life. The aromas of the worldly food were intoxicating.

I had a great time at the pallet shop. It allowed me to converse with English outsiders, and it was where I started planning my escape, which I aimed to execute when I turned eighteen. The shop was equipped with power tools, air compressors, band saws—everything operated by electricity. It was full of worldly people and their worldly influence. Inside the building was a forklift—a forbidden luxury in the Amish world—that I longed to use. I imagined myself driving that forklift, flying through the shop with stacks of pallets, moving them from place to place, or loading the big trucks that carried them away. My brother and I did simple tasks, like stacking, sorting, and sweeping. But these simple tasks were a tremendous help in building my confidence and self-esteem.

This experience, like our horse-training venture, didn't last long. Other Amish church members discovered that my brother and I were working at the pallet shop, which led to the bishops convening a meeting with my dad. They threatened to excommunicate my dad from the church if he didn't immediately remove us from the pallet shop. They believed that the worldly people and environment would negatively influence us. They were concerned that we could be tempted to use power tools—which they believed could lead us to Hell—or that we might ride forklifts—another path to damnation. Little did they know how eagerly I aspired to do all those things. They claimed they were close enough to hear the radio playing worldly music inside the building, confirming that we were also exposed to forbidden music. After the meeting with the bishops, our father informed us that we had to quit working there.

I was devastated by the loss. I was once again cut off from the world and confined to what seemed like a prison. Although I didn't know it at the time, my introduction to the pallet shop opened a door into my future.

23

MUSIC

I really liked the worldly music I'd heard while working at the pallet shop. I gave money to one of our English driver friends to buy me a headset to listen to more of it. He taught me to insert a cassette tape to listen to music or switch to FM radio for local stations. Before I made the purchase, he assured me it would be compact enough to hide discreetly. He brought it to me once I had saved some money from my earnings at the pallet shop. Unknown to Mom and Dad, I had set aside some cash to buy personal items.

Listening to worldly music brought me comfort, and I enjoyed it until my brother discovered the cassette player and smashed it on the concrete. He was far more loyal to the church's strict rules than I was. He even threatened to tell our parents. I distinctly recall the horror and devastation I felt when my headset was found and destroyed the first time. It ignited an anger within me. I was furious and thought, 'You won't take my music away from me.' On days when I was feeling low and deeply depressed, I needed to listen to music. It was my way of coping with a life I desperately wanted to escape, but I lacked the resources to save myself. Music was my coping mechanism, and it had been taken from me.

I gave the driver more money for another cassette player and head-set. This cycle occurred several times. Sometimes, the English driver even chipped in and helped me buy a replacement if I didn't have enough money. He made sure I got another cassette player every time mine was found and broken. I'd find new hiding spots, in the barn, under a bale of hay, or some other place on the farm—farms have plenty of hiding spots. Every opportunity I had, I'd break free and listen to music in the hayloft near the roof's peak. Sometimes, I'd sneak out to the barn late at night while everyone was asleep, put on my headset, and get lost in the music of Willie Nelson, George Jones, Conway Twitty, and Dolly Parton.

Music filled me with hope. It reminded me that there was a world beyond my own. A place existed where I could be happy, and it held the promise that I might escape to be part of it someday and listen to those tunes freely without regulations or fear.

24

THE ABUSE CONTINUED

I have vivid memories of the physical abuse that occurred in my family when I was a young Amish child. Most notable were the times my father beat my mother while he was in a drunken rage. My siblings and I watched in terror as my father strangled her. We were always instructed not to reach out to the English world—those "scary, worldly people." We were told that any issues or problems needed to be addressed within the church. We trusted that my mother reported everything to the church leaders as she should have. We understood that what our father was doing was wrong, especially when we saw him break down the door with a sledge-hammer and proceed to choke and hit her.

As we grew older, the physical abuse expanded to include my twin brother and me, usually in retaliation for some mistakes we made. One time, I accidentally threw a shovel into the granary while my father was cleaning it. I had no idea he was inside at the time. It was a monthly chore to clean it out to prevent too much grain from sticking to the sides as it flowed down on an angle. The door had latched shut because of the wind, and I didn't realize what had happened. When I opened the door and threw the shovel inside, it hit my father, and he became enraged. He stormed out and found my twin brother and I on a wagon. He grabbed both of us and violently slammed our heads together. We both fell to the ground, unconscious.

Years later, my mother mentioned how that incident affected my decision to leave the Amish. It left a lasting impact on her because she witnessed the rage from the house. Mom revealed that both my brother and I likely suffered concussions. We were told we would receive a spanking if we didn't return to work immediately, so we had no choice but to endure severe headaches and nausea while continuing with our chores. If we hadn't, we risked facing another round of beatings.

Another time I was on top of the silo tossing silage down to feed the cows when I suddenly heard a commotion. I turned to see my father and older brother in a heated argument. My father began physically beating my brother, and I could hear his agonizing screams. But what terrified me most was the sight of my father wielding a two-by-four and relentlessly striking my brother all over his head and body. I could hear the sickening crunch as it made contact. I had seen my father kill animals in a similar fashion many times and I honestly feared that he was killing my brother. I once saw him use a hammer to kill a cat and witnessed him club a dog to death on several occasions, so this wasn't an unfamiliar sight. But when I saw it happen to my brother, I knew I had to do something quickly.

I rushed down the silo as quickly as I could to distract my father, and he chased after me as I had hoped. I managed to evade him by hiding behind a wall of hay bales in the barn and entering through a tunnel I had previously created. My father was unaware of the tunnel's existence and couldn't find me. When he eventually did locate me, he beat me for interfering in what he called "discipline." I firmly believe that if I hadn't intervened, my brother might not have survived that day.

I witnessed my father's wrath on other occasions as well. One day, my younger brother playfully threw an apple across the road, trying to hit one of the passing semi-trucks. My father became so enraged that he grabbed my little brother by the ear and then by his hair, inflicting tremendous pain. His screams and desperate pleas still haunt me to this day.

As we aged, we learned from English people that if we went to the neighbors and called 911, the police would come and arrest our father. It provided us with temporary relief from the abuse. We did this several times, and my father ended up with five domestic violence offenses that resulted in him being detained in jail for a short period. Although this put a temporary stop to the violence, my father grew angrier after each release. The sheriff's department saw my mother's bruises and could plainly see what was going on, but she would always say, "No, we're Amish, and we don't press charges."

In one particularly painful incident, my father disciplined me using a paddle on my rear, which was a common and acceptable form of punishment. However, when I instinctively put my hand back there because of the pain, he didn't stop. He was so infuriated by my attempt to relieve my misery that he began hitting my knuckles until they bled. I had to shift the pain from one place to another so it wouldn't continue to hurt my rear. Once my knuckles started bleeding, I let go, and he resumed hitting me on my rear. He hurt me so badly that I couldn't sit for a very long time.

On some Sundays, when I attended the church service—where we sat on hard wooden benches that were uncomfortable enough on their own—I found myself unable to sit due to the pain. I walked around the barn to visit with the horses during most of the church service. But when my father discovered my frequent trips to the barn, he beat me for being outside too long.

These relentless beatings were a motivating force behind my desire to leave the Amish community. I believed my only options were to eliminate myself through death, suicide, or escape, even though all these choices would condemn me to Hell. I had been brainwashed to think that leaving the Amish faith would lead me to eternal damnation, but I felt that facing the Devil in Hell would be better than enduring the hellish life I was trapped in on Earth. Throughout my teenage years, the feeling of eventual and eternal damnation persisted. When I finally left the Amish, I couldn't shake the belief that I was destined for Hell. But I was willing to take that chance to escape my immediate suffering.

25

SINKING INTO DEPRESSION

The pallet shop had been my refuge, where I could find solace and regain my sanity. While the Amish church pretended to be concerned for our souls, they also feared we might start earning too much money. In our Old Order Amish community, making money was a competitive sport among families. If someone believed another family was becoming more financially successful, they voiced their "concerns" to the church's elders and bishop. If there was agreement that someone was earning too much money, they would act to rein in their earning because you were not allowed to outpace others financially. Even though we were the poorest family in the entire community, there was an incentive to keep us the most impoverished family, and that's just the way it was.

When my father pulled us out of the pallet shop, I knew then that I would leave the Amish, regardless of the consequences or the hardships I might face. As a teenager, I was overwhelmingly unhappy and desperate to escape. Working at the pallet shop meant if my father had a bad day or got drunk, he couldn't physically abuse or beat me. It served as a haven from the turmoil and abuse at home.

In the non-Amish world, I had a taste of freedom. I was surrounded by people who loved and accepted me, who smiled at me and offered their help. It was an entirely different experience from everything I had known. I didn't feel like an outcast and wasn't subjected to bullying and rejection at the pallet shop. I had many true friends there.

The pallet shop was the place I hatched my escape plan about two years before leaving. I became friends with Blake, who later played a pivotal role in helping me when I turned eighteen. I maintained contact with Blake until I was old enough to leave. I was initially skeptical and feared he might eventually disappoint me, but he never did. He promised not to reveal my plans to anyone, and he kept his word. I asked him not to inform my parents because I knew they would try to stop me from leaving.

I had serious thoughts about leaving as early as twelve years old. It seemed like an impossible goal at that age, but as time moved forward, I became more resolute in my determination to make it happen, one way or another.

The loss of my job at the pallet shop plunged me into a deep depression and desperation. It was a blind desperation that ultimately enabled me to walk away from the only life I had ever known, even if the price was eternal damnation.

26

THE AMISH GRAPEVINE

The speed at which gossip circulated in my Amish community was astounding. Gossip traveled faster than the news delivered by a phone call. In our Amish community, there was a tradition that when you heard something worth sharing, you'd hitch up your horse and buggy and visit each house to spread the word. This was our primary means of communication since we had no phones. Some New-Order Amish had phone shacks, but we weren't permitted to have those. So, when we heard something newsworthy, we hitched up our horse and buggy to spread the word.

The grapevine system was so effective that by Sunday, everyone already knew what had happened in every single family during the past week. If it was a topic of interest, the entire community was well-informed about the happenings in each family. Whether it was a tragic event or someone violating Amish rules before the bishop and elders could bring it up in church, word quickly spread throughout the community. People were willing to pause their busy days and distribute news to neighbors who would continue spreading it to other Amish families.

When our barn burned down during my fifth-grade year, every member of the community was aware of it before Sunday's service. There wasn't a single person who hadn't heard the news. When someone left the Amish, horses and buggies hit the road. They went from house to house, informing everyone that so-and-so had a son or daughter who had left the Amish and was now destined for Hell. This type of news spread like wildfire, with each retelling adding more details. Even if it wasn't true, it still circulated. People talked about one another, belittled one another, and made unfounded claims about each other without bothering to verify the accuracy of the information. This was particularly true if someone challenged the church or had been shunned. They would gossip about that person's supposed wrongdoing, how they were different, and so on; it was tribalism at its worst.

27

YOUTH GROUP

Youth group is a significant event in the life of an Amish teenager. I looked forward to it based on what I had heard from the older kids who joined the youth group at the age of seventeen. Unlike other Amish groups practicing Rumspringa, which allows a period of running around and exploring the world, we were not allowed to do anything like that. Instead, we had our youth group; you had to be seventeen to join. On Sunday nights, we gathered at someone's house to sing songs, and dating was allowed. However, you couldn't ask a girl out directly—that was considered prideful. Instead, you had to have a friend or brother ask a girl on a date for you.

I had high expectations for the youth group. They all seemed confident and important, dressed in crisp homemade clothing. Everyone had their own German songbook, which was a badge of honor. I thought I would finally be respected after joining the youth group.

But it didn't turn out as I had hoped. I experienced more bullying and backlash because I wanted to be a typical teenager and have some fun. I got into trouble for not following the strict dress code. I sometimes left my collar open or neglected to button the last button of my shirt up to my neck. Our dress code was unique even among the Amish, and I pushed the boundaries by having my cousin make me a shirt with a three-inch cuff on the sleeve, even though the dress code allowed only an inch and a half. When I wore that shirt to youth group, people openly discussed my shirt right in front of me. I enjoyed the attention and didn't mind stirring things up. But my dad eventually told me to stop wearing the shirt because he was going to be shunned by the church if I continued to violate the dress code.

I also refused to date any girls. While my twin brother immediately started dating, I held back from dating because I knew I was going to leave the Amish. I had already made up my mind that nothing would stop me. I didn't want a romantic relationship to keep me from pursuing my desire for freedom, happiness, and peace. It didn't mean I didn't have crushes on a few girls; there were a couple I could have dated if I had planned to stay Amish. One of the girls I admired the most also happened to be a first cousin.

In our Amish community, we were discouraged from dating outside our church community, even if it meant dating a first cousin. They preferred us to marry within our community rather than date someone from a more modernized Amish church with fewer rules. Violating our ordinance was discouraged while breaking state laws was tolerated. The emphasis was on adhering to our church's rules and ordinances to please God, even if it meant going against government laws. For instance, we were not allowed to use battery-powered lights on our buggies for night safety, even though this is what the law required. Orange was deemed satanic; therefore, this belief superseded the state law requiring a reflective orange triangle on the rear of unpowered vehicles at night. In case you don't already know, buggies are all black—flat black—and virtually invisible in the dark.

Some individuals did choose to date people from New-Order Amish communities, which had more modern practices. However, they faced criticism and sometimes even shunning from our church. Those who did so knew they would have to marry into the other community and stay there, as returning home would result in a severe backlash from the church. They would need to seek forgiveness and face consequences for straying from our traditional Amish way of life if they ever wanted to return.

The whole Youth Group experience was disappointing but not surprising. It further served to emphasize that I had no future within my Old-Order Amish community; I didn't want them, and they sure didn't want me.

28

BREAKING AMISH RULES

Breaking Amish rules became a source of bonding and adventure for my father and me. I had some good times with my father despite describing so much abuse. It's possible to love and hate a person at the same time. Love and hate are not opposites; they're both expressions of passion. The opposite of love and hate is simply apathy—not caring.

Although I can say I hated my father when he abused my mother, siblings, and me, I also wanted his love, and I wanted to love him. My father's situation was complex. His nature was equal parts abusive and fun-loving, which was at odds with his Amish surroundings. I'm not excusing anything he did, but he had two distinctly different sides, one I hated, the other I loved; this is the dilemma abuse victims face.

Our rule-breaking adventures are some of the fondest memories I have of him. Often, he was already shunned by the church for minor violations, usually related to the dress code, so he was less concerned about getting into more trouble. These unchecked moments of freedom provided a welcome break from the over-whelming constraints of our Amish life.

One day my dad, already under the influence of alcohol, made me an irresistible proposition: "You want to break some Amish rules?" he asked. Without hesitation, I agreed, unaware of what he had in mind or what I was about to get myself into. We ended up at The Plaza Inn in Mount Victory, Ohio, which had a private airstrip where small planes landed, bringing people to the restaurant. We sat there, enjoying our meal, while my dad threw back a few beers. Eating in a restaurant was a pretty serious infraction of Amish rules, not to mention the beers. But things were about to get even crazier.

As the beer began to do its work, my father struck up a conversation with a man who happened to own an airplane. To my disbelief, my dad persuaded him to take us on an airplane ride. I was petrified, but I didn't want to show fear in front of my dad, so I bravely went along.

This spontaneous flight was a major transgression in our community because flying was considered a grave sin. It was an act of pride, an attempt to defy the natural order of creation by ascending toward God and Heaven.

As the plane's engine roared, its deafening noise penetrated the protective earmuffs I wore. The acrid smell of exhaust and fuel filled the air as the rickety aircraft vibrated and shook while gaining speed on the uneven grass strip. A sinking feeling rolled through me as the wheels left the ground, and I couldn't help but believe that this was the day I would die. As we climbed toward Heaven, all I could see was the sky from my seat in the rear of the plane. But as we leveled off, my fears gave way to amazement as I looked out the side window to the miniaturized world below.

In the front of the plane, my dad talked with the pilot, their voices muffled by my earmuffs. Slowly, it dawned on me that my dad had persuaded the pilot to fly above our farm. With the plane banking in tight circles, I peered out of the side window, my heart pounding in my chest. To my astonishment, I spotted my younger brother standing in front of our barn, waving cheerfully at the airplane overhead. Little did he know that his brother Eli and his dad were aboard that airplane. That was a moment that I'll never forget.

Years later, after leaving the Amish community, I shared this story with my brother, who initially doubted me until I described what he did in detail. He remembered the day the airplane flew in tight circles above our farm. Our adventures in rule-breaking, like this airplane ride, created a unique bond between my father and me. Our adventures into the English world allowed us momentary freedom from the constraints of the Amish church, and they brought rare moments of laughter and joy.

On another occasion, my dad had been in trouble with the church for several weeks. When Dad was drinking heavily, he had hangovers each morning. He slept late and was often quite difficult to handle. Mom went to great lengths to ensure that we boys were occupied on the farm or elsewhere in the Amish community so we were out of his sight before he went to work. But Dad caught on to what she was doing, and one day he found me and demanded that I go with him to his job. I was struggling with depression at the time, and while I dreaded being with my father, I was also desperate for a relationship with the part of him that I loved. When he wanted me to go with him, I didn't bother to tell Mom that he had pulled me off my fencing project, even though I was far behind. We had to get the fence put in before fall so we could turn the animals loose to graze. But he demanded I go with him that day, saying he needed some help. I just said, "Okay, Dad," and did as he asked.

He had some beer in the buggy that he brought to the barn where we were working. We were up on the roof removing some old, rusty metal sheets that needed to be replaced with new ones. He had been drinking throughout the time, joking like he often did when he was feeling good. He talked smack about the bishop and the elders, which, for me, was very funny. I already knew all the rules and regulations because I was preparing for baptism, and the church leaders were riding me pretty hard, too. When I heard Dad talk about the bishops, deacons, and church leaders, using some choice German cuss words, I just laughed and laughed. I loved it. I was feeding off his good mood and responded with some even worse cuss words that made him laugh in return.

After we'd removed about half of the metal roofing, Dad was looking down inside this English guy's barn and said, "There's a dirt bike down there. I wonder if that thing runs." He just mentioned it in passing, and then we went back to working on the roof. We were enjoying working together and talking. Some old memories came up, and he talked about his mother. He even mentioned that maybe we should leave the Amish and go find her, wherever she was, and we could just live happily ever after. That really tickled my ears because he didn't know my secret desire to leave the Amish. I thought, 'Wow, Dad, I know you're laughing and joking when you say it, you're probably not serious.'

Lunchtime rolled around. It was about noon. Mom always packed sandwiches for him. We had our own homemade meats that we put in jars, called liverwurst (leberwurst). Dad said, "Well, my packed lunch is big enough for us both. Let's eat lunch inside the house."

The English guy that we were working for had gone to a meeting. He was involved with some local government affairs and said we could come into the house for a break while he was gone. We had the house all to ourselves.

Dad drank some more beer during lunch, turned the television on, and flipped through a couple of channels. I was impressed by his expertise with the worldly television set, going from one channel to another. That was all foreign to me. I realized that he'd done this before because he knew exactly what he was doing. It was a Saturday, and they were showing motorsports with dirt bikes going over a series of little hills. Then they'd turn a sharp curve and race each other to see who's going to be the winner. I was instantly drawn to it, but it lasted only about twenty minutes.

When lunch was over, Dad said, "That was so amazing. I'm going to go try that right now on that motorcycle in the barn."

I said, "Dad, no, no, no, no. You've been drinking. You might get killed." But he was determined, as always. I didn't argue because that would have quickly escalated into anger and rage, so as usual, I just tried to keep him calm. "Okay, Dad, if that's what you want to do," like the airplane incident, I just went with the flow.

He went out to the barn. It probably took a half hour, and how he got that motorcycle running is beyond me. I was surprised the English guy didn't come back and catch us. He kept working the kickstarter over and over, and finally, it sputtered to life. It coughed and sneezed, but gradually ran more steady as white smoke poured out of the exhaust pipe. He kept revving it up to work the old gas out of it. Eventually, he wheeled it out behind the barn into an open field. Partway into the field, there was a dip and then a rise upward. It wasn't like we saw on television. On the television, the hills were short and abrupt. This was a much longer slope. I didn't think he'd get much speed, so I wasn't too worried about him getting airborne. I thought, 'Well, whatever happens, happens. It is what it is. Let Dad have some fun. I just hoped he didn't ask me to get on that thing.'

He mounted the dirt bike as I stood back and watched as he started across the field. The dirt bike was loud, and he kept revving the engine. Then he took off like a shot. I had no idea that thing would go so fast. He twisted the throttle to the max and never let go, never hit the brakes. Through the cloud of exhaust, I watched him head full speed for that dip and hill. I could smell the fumes from the wake of exhaust as it swirled around me. He was going faster than the cars I had seen on the road. He was just flying!

I quickly realized his intent. He was heading full speed for the dip and then up the hill. He was going to show me that he could do what they had done on the television. And boy, did he ever. He hit the dip and shot up the hill. I saw his Amish hat fly off, and his long beard was plastered to both sides of his neck, proving to me that he had some serious speed. I was thinking, 'This is going to be bad.' As he came to the top of the hill, he and the dirt bike went airborne and parted company. My father was higher in the air than the dirt bike. Then they both disappeared from view, followed by a sickening crunch.

I took off running. As I ran to find him, I remember thinking, 'How am I going to explain this to the church? What do I do if he's hurt badly? He could be dead. What will I tell my mother and my siblings?' All these fears raced through my mind as I ran toward the top of the hill.

As I crested the hill, nothing could have prepared me for the sight before me. The dirt bike had veered to the left and crashed into some trees. It was lying there, jerking and sputtering like a dying beast. One of the wheels was completely twisted off. What remained of the dirt bike was pretty much a mangled piece of metal groaning in the throes of death.

To the right, and not quite as far as the dirt bike, was my father, sitting in the grass, hands raised in hysterical laughter. He looked up at me and said, "That was awesome!"

"Dad, are you okay?" I asked.

"Yeah, I'm okay."

"You never hit the brake!" I exclaimed.

"I didn't know where the brake was, but I sure found the throttle! The throttle was all I needed. That was awesome. I was way up in the air. Did you see that?"

I replied, "Dad, I saw that, but are you sure you're okay? You hit the ground pretty hard and rolled quite a ways. Are you sure you don't have broken bones?"

He dismissed my concern and said, "I feel fine. I had enough beer to feel pretty good. Let's go back up to the barn and do some more drinking!"

Then the English guy came home. My dad was extremely polite and apologetic to the English man and simply explained everything, confessed everything that happened, and even said how much fun he'd had. I think the man was stunned to the point he could hardly believe what he was seeing and hearing. Dad assured the English man, before he could get upset, and said, "My son and I will work for you however long it takes to pay for that dirt bike."

The man was a little upset at first because he had wanted to sell the dirt bike since he hadn't ridden it in a while. Someone had offered him $1200 for it, so we settled on that as a value, even though he might have been able to get more. But he said that he appreciated our honesty. So my dad and I worked for free for quite a while. Sometimes I wasn't with him, but he worked for several more weeks to make sure that he paid it off. It was a great day and a favorite memory, outside of the airplane incident.

Amazingly, nobody ever found out. Looking back, I remember being so afraid of how I would explain this to the church and the family. But nobody ever said anything. I'm amazed at how tough my dad was. Being drunk might have helped in several ways. When he hit the ground, I believe he just rolled like a sack of feed. I saw him do other crazy stuff when he was drunk, and he always came out unscathed. I was amazed that he was not hurt, but I was even more amazed that the story never got him shunned. Nobody within the community ever found out. No family knew about it, either. It remained a secret between my father and me.

We continued to find opportunities to defy Amish rules together, like driving tractors or trucks. We bonded over these moments of rule-breaking and enjoyed the shared excitement and laughter. My father's relaxed attitude during these times provided a rare and precious sense of connection and happiness that I treasured. These memories remain dear to me and have become an important part of my testimonies on social media. Those moments made me feel almost "normal."

Given my father's rule-breaking history, it seemed natural for me to follow in his footsteps. I knew he didn't take the church rules seriously, and I questioned why I should. I began to defy church authority with greater boldness.

I continued to defy Amish rules on my own. One pivotal incident involved riding a bicycle, an act deemed too worldly by the Amish religious leaders. This bicycle incident, ironically, became a critical incentive for my decision to leave the Amish community.

I was caught riding a bicycle, and this seemingly innocent act led to the shocking verdict that I no longer qualified for baptism. I was dumbfounded by the notion that I was destined for Hell simply because of a bicycle.

This marked a turning point for me. While I had always desired to leave, I had not yet experienced a decisive moment that pushed me toward action. The absurdity of being condemned to Hell for riding a bicycle changed that.

Frustrated and disenchanted, I confronted the church leaders, questioning their stance. I pointed out that other Amish communities allowed bicycles just a short distance away, and some even believed it pleased God. Yet, according to my church, I was condemned to eternal damnation for riding one.

Their standard response was, "That's our ordinance; you must follow it." But that was no longer enough for me. The random nature of their rules and the lack of consistency embittered me, and I resented their yearning for control over my life.

I openly confronted their hypocrisy and let them shun me. I no longer cared.

Around the age of fourteen, my father gave me a diary. It seemed an odd thing at the time, quite out of character. But he said his father had given one to him, and he wanted to honor the tradition.

This diary became an outlet for my experiences and frustrations, including the rule-breaking adventures with my father and my personal struggles. In this diary, I poured out my honest feelings, often in profane and vulgar terms; I held nothing back.

Amish culture dictates that we suppress emotions and refrain from sharing our feelings. It demanded that I become a stoic and unwavering man from a young age. As I transitioned from childhood to adulthood, I learned to bury my emotions deep within myself.

I chronicled not only the rule-breaking adventures but also the physical abuse I endured from my father and the bullying I faced in school and at church, along with the malicious gossip that flowed throughout our community and the baseless rumors intended to break my spirit. I left nothing to the imagination.

Little did I know then that this diary would play an important role in reshaping my relationship with my father in the coming years.

29

GOD

As a teenager, I was afraid of God. Mainly because I thought He'd be really mad at me for leaving the Amish community. Honestly, I didn't give God much thought other than to fear Him and didn't clearly understand who He was. When I left, my image of God was mostly that He'd be furious because I'd broken away from the system that taught me that being Amish was the only way to reach Heaven. I genuinely believed that was the only path to Heaven, even though I couldn't follow all their strict rules. It felt like I was caught in a trap with no way to escape.

I didn't really know God at all. I had a good grasp of religious teachings and the Amish way of life, but God remained an abstract concept. Words like *salvation* meant nothing to me because our group never discussed such things. Instead, we were taught that salvation came from following the Amish church's rules. You'd end up in Hell if you didn't follow those rules.

Even during funerals, the conversations centered around the dead person's alignment with the church's ordinance as the basis for their hope of reaching Heaven. I never heard anyone say something like, "I believe they're going to Heaven because they had faith in Jesus Christ, and that's how we know they'll be in Heaven." Nope, that was never discussed. What I did hear was their optimism for the person in the casket because they had adhered to the church's standards and had been granted forgiveness by a congregational vote before their passing. They were seen as holy individuals because they complied with the ordinance, followed the rules, and received the church's approval.

When someone who hadn't received forgiveness passed away during the shunning period, their burial arrangement depended on their actions. They might be laid to rest separate from others, often in a distant corner or away from the rest of the community. There seemed to be no hope for those who departed without being granted forgiveness or without a congregational vote of pardon. They would be buried far from the "holy" individuals because there was a belief that when Jesus returned, only those who upheld the ordinance and were considered "holy" would be allowed into Heaven. Perhaps they kept these individuals separate to avoid any confusion on Jesus' part about who was deserving of Heaven. The arrogance of such beliefs is truly striking.

I was more afraid of the church than I was of God. When push came to shove, the church held my behavior in check. They were the ones who launched investigations whenever rumors or accusations were flying around, to look into who said and did what. The church was the authority figure and always on someone's case. The deacon would ask questions like, "Hey, is what we heard true? We heard this and that." As a teenager, my fear was squarely directed at the church far more than it was at God. That's just how things played out.

During our formative years, it's natural to shape our perception of God based on the authority figures around us. If someone grows up in a caring and supportive environment, they likely envision God as loving and nurturing. In my case, my view of God resembled that of a crotchety old man who seemed to want Heaven all to himself. It appeared He had orchestrated a world filled with cosmic booby-traps designed to disqualify people from ever reaching Heaven.

Many years later, I stumbled upon a surprising revelation when I read the Bible. I discovered the incredible provision God had made to allow us to become a part of His family and share in an eternity alongside Him. But it's important to note that, at this stage in my story, I was still many years from reaching that understanding.

30

ALONE IN THE WOODS

I never dared to speak about my depression or the overwhelming issues weighing me down. I poured my thoughts and feelings into the diary my father had given me. During my teenage years, the daily impact of my dad's abusive, alcohol-fueled behavior sat upon my emotions like a heavy weight. As my eighteenth birthday approached, the absence of coherent answers to my questions about why we adhered to such a strict Amish lifestyle only deepened my depression. Both situations created an unshakeable sense of futility and hopelessness. It didn't make sense to me that we lived by these strict rules when many other Amish didn't follow them to the same degree. As my despair and hopelessness intensified, I grabbed my rifle and my faithful dog, Betsy, and ventured deep into the woods. I intended to stay there for several weeks in search of a glimmer of solace.

Thankfully, we had a large wooded area behind our farm. I ventured deep into the heart of it, until I reached a point about a mile inside. It was an enormous expanse of woods that connected with one of the English wooded areas. Although I wasn't on our property, I knew I had gone far enough to avoid being discovered. I set up a makeshift tent, covering it with leaves and plastic bags I had brought. I hid out in that tent while understanding that I would face punishment and discipline upon return. But I believed it would be worth it to find some peace for a couple of weeks.

The woods were alive with the cheerful chorus of birdsong. My days were spent hunting squirrels and rabbits and cooking their meat over a small fire. I can still recall the distinct earthy aroma of leaves and the sweet smell of hickory wood that I chopped into pieces with my rusty axe. I used that axe for chopping wood and bringing down small dead trees to fuel my fires. The birds, chirping and conversing with me, were my constant companions. Rain was no bother; my makeshift tent kept me dry. I thrived in this environment, even when thunderstorms rolled in—I felt protected. My upbringing equipped me with the skills to survive off the land, and I used those skills effectively.

After approximately two weeks of hiding in the woods, the harsh realities of my long-term situation began to weigh heavily on my mind. I couldn't remain hidden in the woods indefinitely, especially with winter approaching., I was troubled by the thoughts of what my family must have been going through in my absence. I felt a tinge of guilt over what I was putting my family through.

Reluctantly, I made the decision to return home, knowing I would have to face the consequences of my actions. What awaited me was a blistering butt-beating from my father, who was furious mostly because I hadn't left a note explaining where I'd gone. Astonishingly, my family seemed more concerned about the possibility of me leaving the Amish church than they were about my safety and well-being.

The solitude I had enjoyed during those weeks rejuvenated my mental resilience and fortitude. It provided me with the courage to seriously consider the overwhelming leap I would soon take, like stepping off a figurative cliff. I knew I was about to take a leap of faith that would either usher in a new chapter of life or seal my fate.

31

___

PREPARING TO LEAVE

For many years, leaving the Amish community seemed utterly impossible. Early on, I knew I needed to connect with outsiders to find people who could help me. However, reaching out was extremely risky, as betrayal could send me into an even worse situation at home and within the Amish community at large. Nevertheless, the weight of my pain and desperation drove me to take the risk. I believed that if I explained my circumstances to the right person, someone out there might comprehend what I was enduring and be willing to help me make the break. And so, that's precisely what I did.

As a young teenager, I had mustered the courage to reach out to several English drivers for their assistance. Unfortunately, one of them ended up betraying my trust by sharing our conversation with my dad, which resulted in me receiving a painful spanking. This experience made me wary of trusting anyone close to my Amish family, fearing they might expose my plans. Yet, despite my caution, my desperation drove me forward to find a sympathetic and trustworthy rescuer. I found that person in Blake through my time at the pallet shop. Blake was willing to see past the ties he had with my family and the local Amish community to extend a helping hand to me.

When I was sixteen, I poured my heart out to Blake, tears streaming down my face as I bared my soul to him. He made me a promise, one that would become my lifeline, but with a crucial condition—I had to wait until I turned eighteen. Blake was reluctant to risk getting into trouble and possibly face jail time for helping a minor. I understood the need for caution and knew I had to bide my time until the opportune moment arose. Still, having the assurance of a way out provided me with a glimmer of hope that sustained me.

I grappled with a whirlwind of emotions in the year leading up to my escape. Leaving behind the familiar, even if it was a miserable existence, was an incredibly frightening prospect. There's a strange sense of comfort in familiarity, no matter how oppressive the situation may be.

I held serious doubts about my ability to go through with my escape plan. Over the years, my grandfather, the bishop, along with other church leaders, constantly drilled into me the peril of entertaining beliefs that differed from the Amish faith. They harshly indoctrinated us with the dire warning that leaving the Amish religion would condemn us to the depths of Hell from which there was no escape. It was a persuasive message, one that left a deep mark and was incredibly difficult to shake off—a lingering cloud of religious guilt. Looking back, I can now see it for what it truly was: a form of brainwashing.

The disturbing accounts of those who had left for New-Order Amish communities only to meet tragic ends in car accidents or other calamities remained in the forefront of my mind. According to the religious leaders, these accidents were God's judgment for leaving the Amish faith. These stories, combined with the fear-inducing Sunday church services that warned of the pitfalls of the English world, sent shivers down my spine and nearly stopped me from pursuing my escape plan. At times, the fear was so overwhelming that I contemplated discussing my situation with my twin brother or my closest Amish friends. But deep down, I knew that if I confided in them and they betrayed my trust, I could find myself shipped off to an Amish counseling facility for reprogramming. Those facilities were known for their willingness to use medication to break a person down emotionally and physically, all to force them to submit to the Amish religion.

While I genuinely believed that leaving the Amish would lead me straight to Hell, my mindset at the time was rather peculiar. I actually thought it might be worth it to face damnation if it meant experiencing a fleeting taste of freedom before my inevitable descent into eternal torment. It might sound unsettling, but that's the perspective I held back then. In truth, the torment of my existence within the Amish community was so intense that it outweighed my fear of the hell that might await in the afterlife. I was willing to take my chances with God or the Devil, whichever the case may be.

32

MY ESCAPE

As my eighteenth birthday drew near, I had another conversation with Blake, confirming my desire to leave and his commitment to helping me. His response was unwavering: "Yes, I'm serious." However, he also offered the suggestion, "But perhaps we should discuss this with your father. I have great respect for him. I don't want him to be left heartbroken or assume you've gone missing or been kidnapped."

I quickly responded, "No, no, no. He'll find out eventually, and I'll be the one to explain things to him. Just please don't tell him before you come to pick me up." I was well aware of how such conversations typically played out within the Amish community. I had heard stories of how church leaders had confronted individuals wanting to leave, resorting to fear, intimidation, and brainwashing techniques. More often than not, their tactics were highly effective in discouraging people from leaving. I had no desire to subject myself to their manipulation, deceit, and confrontations. I preferred to leave subtly, and if Mom and Dad approached me afterward, I'd explain my reasons. But I had no intention of engaging with the Amish religious authorities on their terms.

I reached the age of eighteen in September 1998, and with that legal milestone, it was time to get serious about planning my escape. I knew I needed to save some money first. I had learned from the English folks that, at eighteen, I was legally considered an adult. So, I took a job at the pallet shop despite my parents' objections. To keep them somewhat content, I decided to share half of the money I earned with them, withholding about $250 for myself. It was just enough to get me started on my journey toward a new life.

My departure was carefully planned for October 11—a church Sunday. That morning at milking time, I declared that I didn't feel well. Not feeling well wasn't a sufficient excuse for not going to church, but it set the stage for my deception. In our community, it was customary for the Youth Group members to be the last to arrive at church. That morning, as everyone prepared to leave, I persuaded Levi to let Alvin go ahead, saying I needed a few extra minutes due to my ailment. Once Alvin departed, I confided in Levi that I felt too unwell to attend church. He warned me about the consequence of missing a church service, but I insisted that my condition was severe enough to justify the risk of punishment. Reluctantly, Levi left without me, leaving me alone and just one step away from my escape.

I had arranged to meet Blake at the pallet shop to avoid any chance of him possibly encountering one of my family members. The morning was sunny and cool; there wasn't a cloud in the sky, and the leaves were starting to display their colors. As the screen door slammed shut behind me for the last time, I walked away from my home. In my possession, I carried a lone cardboard box containing a few prized items. Among them were German songbooks and my German Bible. However, I had unintentionally left behind a significant item: my diary. Armed with these meager belongings and the clothes on my back, I directed my steps toward the pallet shop.

As I walked steadily toward my destiny, an overwhelming urge gnawed at me, tempting me to turn around and steal one last glance at my home. I resisted the temptation and maintained focus on Blake's parked car as I moved ahead with determination. A whirlwind of conflicting emotions churned inside of me. The exhilaration of newfound freedom was thrilling, yet a giant knot of fear tightened in my stomach. It was an indescribable mix of feelings. This was a moment I had envisioned countless times during my teenage years, and now it was unfolding before my eyes—or so it seemed. In some ways, it felt like a dream. I couldn't tear my gaze away from Blake's parked car as the distance between us continued to shrink with each step. All the while, I couldn't help wondering if Blake was inside, waiting for me as he had promised. I kept walking closer and closer, straining to see if someone was sitting in the car. And there he was.

In some ways, my story reminds me of the Israelites' escape from Egypt after years of captivity. I wonder if they experienced something like what I did that morning. I didn't have to cross the Red Sea with the Egyptian army in hot pursuit, but Blake felt like my guide to the Promised Land like Moses was to the Israelites.

Once I settled into the car, Blake's first question was whether I had told my parents. I knew it was important to him that I had shared the truth with them, but it was more important to me that they remained unaware of my plans. So, I resorted to a convenient lie. "Yes," I told Blake.

As we drove away from my old life, the reality of my escape began to sink in. I started to feel a sense of eager anticipation—I was finally free. I was gone for good; I had finally taken the step I had imagined for so many years. There was no turning back, and I was willing to do whatever it took to safeguard my newfound freedom.

One of the first stops Blake made was at a hair salon to get my first-ever haircut. As I watched my long hair—an outward symbol of my Amish identity—fall in clumps to the floor, I thought to myself, 'This is what going to Hell feels like.'

Our next stop was the Goodwill store to buy new clothes. I had never owned store-bought clothing before, and Blake gently steered me away from a pair of women's jeans that caught my eye. Donating my Amish attire to the Goodwill trashcan was both a practical choice and a symbolic gesture of the life I was leaving behind.

We stopped at Kmart to buy some fancy new worldly underwear with genuine elastic! I also got a toothbrush and toothpaste so I could start taking care of my teeth.

We arrived at Blake's older farmhouse in the country. The warmth and affection Blake's wife and three daughters showed me was unlike anything I had ever experienced. They wore genuine smiles, shared laughter, and wrapped me in hugs. They even offered me a room with a bed all to myself. Their authentic affection and love were a new and rather uncomfortable experience for me.

Blake's family rallied around me, eager to educate me in the ways of the English world. They showed me where to find food, provided a brief lesson on indoor plumbing (a novelty for me), and began the task of educating me about movies and music. We spent the evening watching Westerns on television, and it felt absolutely glorious.

Their hospitality and warmth made it feel as though I had gained an entirely new family. I cherished the feeling.

Having grown up with 18th-century technology, adjusting to modern conveniences posed some challenges. I sometimes had trouble distinguishing between imagination and reality. I initially thought Western movies were live broadcasts. I had no understanding of the movie-making process. I didn't understand that worldly people built fictitious situations just for fun. But I quickly caught on to the concept of entertainment and embraced it wholeheartedly.

Despite the wonderful day, sleep eluded me that night. The house seemed unbearably loud compared to the dead silence I was accustomed to all my life. My mind raced with thoughts of what it must have been like for my mom, dad, brothers, and sisters to return home from church and discover that I was gone. I wondered about their conversations and thoughts. Did they feel sadness? Were tears shed? I hadn't left to hurt them. There were moments when tears welled up, and the weight of my actions threatened to overwhelm me. With the noise and all these thoughts swirling in my mind, sleep remained far from me.

As the night hours ticked slowly by, I began to find solace in the notion of my newfound freedom. Gone were the days when I would endure beatings. My life would no longer be dictated by stern, bearded men who claimed to speak on behalf of a God who delighted in human suffering. I was free from the relentless farm labor that had once consumed my days. My future held the promise of hope and opportunity. These thoughts brought a subtle smile to my face, and eventually, sleep overtook me.

33

BEGINNINGS AND ENDINGS

The reality of my new situation hit me like a rogue wave when I woke up Monday morning. After only a few hours of restless sleep, it felt disorienting to wake up in a strange place. It was hard to know where to begin. I was expected to go with Blake to work at the pallet shop that day, and he gently reminded me to put on my new English clothes and guided me through the process of readying myself for the day. I couldn't shake the self-consciousness that came with the changes; the new attire and my altered appearance all felt foreign to me. I had ventured into an entirely different world, and doubts about my ability were almost overwhelming.

I acquainted myself with the unfamiliar items in the bathroom: a toothbrush, toothpaste, and worldly deodorant. A sense of doubt came over me as I gazed at my reflection in the mirror. 'What have I done?' I couldn't help but wonder. It was the first time I had seen myself in a bathroom mirror. We never had large mirrors, or even a bathroom growing up.

My mind raced with thoughts of how horrified my mother would be if she saw my transformation. That's when the realization of heading to work at the pallet shop adjacent to my parent's farm hit me. The shop was frequently visited by the Amish, and the thought sent shivers down my spine. I imagined the judgmental looks and harsh words spoken behind my back and, inevitably, to my face. Fear threatened to paralyze me, but excitement and hope caused me to press forward despite my anxiety.

I was used to waking to the pungent smell of wood-smoke and the earthy smells of a family whose livelihood centered around dirt and animals. My new surroundings smelled much different; English people smelled much better! There was a sweet scent of bath soap, floral notes of shampoo, musky undertones of cologne, and the unmistakable freshness of deodorant. Even the laundry, with its lavender-scented detergents, carried an inviting aroma. Everything smelled wonderful!

In my Amish home, morning silence was broken by the sound of our clanging woodstove. My newfound English morning was filled with sounds of worldly music, muffled voices from the television, along with the opening and closing of the refrigerator and beeping of the microwave. The contrast between my past and my present was dramatically evident in those early moments of the day.

The breakfast smells were different. The heavy lingering smell of bacon fat and coffee was replaced with steamy aromas of various breakfast foods being microwaved; the smells were all new and a delight to my senses. As someone used to a hearty cooked break-fast, the casual passing through the kitchen to grab something to eat on the run was quite jarring.

Mom wasn't in the kitchen to make my breakfast; I had to fend for myself. Blake's family showed me where the food was, and I was told to help myself. I didn't have the fortitude to confront the worldly food machines; the lump in my stomach was filling enough.

I rode with Blake to the pallet shop. The first half of our trip passed in total silence. Blake eventually broke the quiet with a simple question: "How do you like your new life?"

I wasn't sure what he expected me to say or even what I should have said. My answer was simply, "I don't know."

He continued by asking me if I was okay. I thought I was, I assumed I was, but truthfully, I didn't really know. Okay is a relative state, and I no longer had a reference point. I had no idea how weird I would feel in this new and strange world. It had all happened so quickly, and I was having difficulty absorbing all the changes, both externally and internally; it was overwhelming.

Blake was very encouraging. He seemed to truly understand and told me, "You'll make it...you'll be fine." At that moment, his words of encouragement meant the world to me.

Although I had worked at the pallet shop before, this day was very different. Everyone looked at me differently. Gone was the separation that had been created by my Amish appearance; now, I looked like one of them. They welcomed me warmly as one might greet a new tribe member. There were lots of compliments and encouragement for my new look. Their acceptance made me feel welcomed, like I belonged.

The owner of the pallet shop was taken aback by my new appearance. I could tell he felt bad for my parents, whom he loved and respected. Any parent hurts when another parent loses a child, regardless of the circumstances.

He immediately began giving me tasks that had previously been off-limits. I wasn't Amish anymore, and I was now eighteen and could legally operate any piece of machinery in the shop. He asked me if I wanted to run the forklift, to which I responded, "ABSOLUTELY!"

The realization of the new opportunities I had ahead of me, and the removal of the prior restrictions thrilled me and helped to lighten my mood. The excitement drowned out the ever-present fear and shame I felt over my choice to leave home.

I could drive the forklift and operate the tear-down machine all by myself! People showed me how to do things I'd never done before. It was so freeing; it's hard for me to describe what this felt like—it was incredible. I could do all these new things without fear of an Amish snitch ratting me out to an Amish Bishop eager to take away the things I enjoyed. This was real, and it didn't have to end!

One of the most amazing things I heard that day was from the pallet shop owner when he told me that now he could pay me more because I could do more things; I was more valuable. That was an eye-opener to me. I'd never thought about my value equating to what I could do and that I could increase my value by learning and doing new things.

Later that morning, I dismounted the forklift to straighten a stack of pallets inside a trailer when one of my coworkers came to me and quietly said, "Hey, Eli, your dad wants to talk to you." With those words, a wave of fear shot through me like electricity. I thought I might die on the spot. I didn't know exactly what he wanted, but I was certain why he had come.

As I stepped out of the trailer and turned the corner, I came face to face with my father. His face showed fatigue and defeat. As my gaze passed over him, I noticed something in his hand; it was my diary. A wave of nausea hit me, thinking about the words I had written in that diary. Words I'd never intended for his ears or any human eyes, words that were my private, unfiltered emotions and expressions, words that would certainly hurt him deeply. As I looked into his eyes, it was obvious that he'd read it.

He looked me over, taking in my changed appearance, before breaking the tense silence. "So, you left the Amish, huh," he said, more as a statement than a question.

I didn't offer an explanation. I simply nodded my confirmation.

His voice was solemn and serious. He told me he wasn't surprised. When the family came home from church the day before, a quick glance at my room and the things that were missing made the conclusion easy. Knowing my affection for the pallet shop, he had come to find me.

He asked me if there was any way to get me to come back home. My answer was firm; I told him I wouldn't be coming back and that I didn't want to be Amish anymore. I braced myself for a lecture or an outburst of rage, but his response took me by surprise. He took responsibility. He had read the diary, and the truthful thoughts he'd read had broken him. He didn't ask me to come back. He simply said that he wished things had been different. He spoke as if he really wanted me to be free, almost as if he admired me for doing something he'd never dared to do. Oddly, I felt that he respected me for the first time. His uncharacteristically gracious response calmed my fears. We cried together and hugged each other. Then, he said something I never expected to hear in my life, "Eli, I want you to know that I love you."

He handed me my diary and excused himself. He told me he knew I had a job to do and didn't want to hold me up. As he turned and walked away, his steps didn't display anger but rather the weight of intense sorrow. The man I had feared all my life now seemed vulnerable, almost frail. His pace was slow, each step heavy as he made his way back home.

As I stood there watching him walk away, I felt an incredible release. It was as if a heavy burden was lifted; a load I didn't even realize I was carrying was gone. With it came a flood of emotions. I looked at the diary in my hand, thinking of the poison it contained. I walked it to the dumpster, never wanting to revisit its pages again in my life.

After my father left, I needed a private moment. I excused myself to the bathroom, where my pent-up emotions finally erupted. Tears streamed down my face; my sobs were uncontrollable. The intensity of my crying was so loud that everyone in the pallet shop could hear. They understood; many had seen and heard my exchange with my dad and were moved to tears themselves.

Soon, a coworker came to the bathroom door to check on me. "Are you okay?" they asked. Through my tears, I managed to reply, "Yes, I'm okay…I'm more than okay. I'm great!" And in that moment, amid the tears, I felt an incredible sense of liberation. I truly felt great.

The following days were an emotional rollercoaster. The feeling of freedom was an indescribable high. At the same time, I felt bad for my dad, and I felt powerless to help him. I felt bad that I'd hurt him, that I'd hurt my mother, brothers, and sisters. Some of my brothers sneaked into the pallet shop, crying and pleading with me to come back. Witnessing their pain was hard. But I remained resolute in my decision; there was no going back.

As time passed, I found an inner strength I didn't know I possessed. I realized I had achieved something my father had longed for himself. Despite the challenges ahead of me, I felt a happiness I had never experienced before. This newfound strength allowed me to face my siblings and other members of the Amish community with grace and confidence. I told them that I was happy, I was going to be okay, and I wasn't coming back.

PART 3

ON MY OWN

34

ADULTING IN THE ENGLISH WORLD

I was free from the Amish world, but it was like I didn't really exist in the eyes of the English world. Many New-Order Amish have Social Security numbers and birth certificates, which make joining the English workforce much easier. Since I didn't have any of these worldly identifiers, I was like a non-person. I knew I existed, but I couldn't prove it without these essential documents. My employer was very accommodating and gave me time to get my sealed birth certificate, social security number, and photo ID—all the things English people have. I had a hard time getting all this sorted—I had no idea how to do it or how long it would take.

Blake went with me to get my photo ID. The people who issued the photo identification said, "Well, you got to have a birth certificate." They wanted me to prove who I was. No one ever questioned who I was before. But I didn't have a birth certificate, so I had to figure out how to get one.

Blake took me to the Health Department for a birth certificate, and they asked, "Where's your ID?"

I explained, "I just tried to get an ID. They told me that I needed a birth certificate. So, I'm here to get a birth certificate."

"We need an ID. We need something that says who you are."

Even though my Amish community was very strict—no government ties, no Social Security numbers, no birth certificates—they did report the birth of newborn babies, including the birthdate, name, and gender. My birth record was in the Health Department's system since 1980, when I was born. I just had to produce something that connected me to the information on the computer.

Among the few items I had taken with me when leaving my parent's home was my second-grade report card. I have no idea why I had that particular report card, but it proved extremely valuable. That second-grade report card was all the Health Department bureaucrats required to connect me with the birth record on the computer. I told them my parents' names, that I am a twin, and my birthdate, and showed them my report card, and that's all I needed! I had my birth certificate within a week. Now, I could finally go to the Social Security Administration and apply for a Social Security number.

It took me nine months after leaving the Amish to work out all these details. It was very frustrating. But at least I was able to work and get paid cash while I worked through the process. Blake really stuck with me.

Blake struggled with me because I wanted to do everything my way and in my own time. He had difficulty getting me to understand that there's a process for everything and rules matter. You can't just go out and start driving a car without insurance. He told me all of that, but I didn't care. I was impatient and had a very low regard for worldly rules. I'm surprised Blake didn't kick me out of his house. He threatened to a few times, and I don't blame him. He didn't, and I eventually left on my own less than a year later.

Blake helped me buy my first car, a 1992 Plymouth Sundance. If you've never heard of a Plymouth Sundance, don't worry, you're not missing anything. I drove the little Sundance when he wasn't around. I had no license, registration, or insurance. That's one of the first boo-boos I made when I left the Amish—driving without a license, insurance, or tags on my car. I bought the car with my own money and figured it was mine to drive, so I did. I think I topped 100 miles an hour on one of the back roads the day I bought it.

Later that same day, I crashed and rolled my car. Since we weren't allowed to have music in the Amish, I was jamming out to the Spice Girls. Thinking back, I have to laugh about my choice in music, the Spice Girls were more of a teen girls' group, but I didn't care. I had that car for less than twenty-four hours when I crashed and rolled onto an Amish guy's property. When everything finally came to a stop, I found myself on the tongue of his manure spreader with that Spice Girls song playing, "Tell me what you want, what you really, really want." It was the only thing I could hear, and I thought, 'I'm not sure what I really want, but I'm pretty sure this isn't it.' The Amish couple on the property came running to help me crawl through the car window while the Spice Girls, at full volume, continued to question me about what I wanted. I finally figured out how to turn the radio off—it was quite humiliating. Adding to my humiliation was the fact the couple knew who I was. I had gone to school with their son.

The car was towed back to Blake's house. No police report was made—none of that kind of thing. I made things right with the farmer and repaired the manure spreader.

Blake gave me a severe talking-to after that incident. He told me, "You better listen to me. You must have insurance, and you need a driver's license. Do not drive without me." I listened to him a little more after that.

When I first left home, I looked like I was free. I looked happy and smiled, but I was deeply troubled in my spirit and soul. It's not easy to function in life when you think you're going to spend eternity in Hell after you die, and I was certain of this reality. Even though I was separated from the Amish church—I had turned eighteen, I was driving a car, and watching television—I remained miserable inside. I had left the Amish, but the Amish hadn't left me. I liked all the new things, but I planned on having fun while I could because I was condemned in the hereafter. That's the way I thought. Only now can I reflect and say what I was honestly thinking. I didn't admit my feelings to anybody at that time, not even to myself, but I seriously believed I had chosen to go to Hell. I couldn't shake that off.

I was blessed to have a friend like Blake to help me transition into worldly ways. I knew nothing and didn't know what I didn't know about the world at large. I'd never even interacted with any New-Order Amish, let alone English people. When I first left, I struggled much worse than someone who'd left other Amish communities. Many other Amish my age had already ventured out into the English world with their family members to conduct business. Many other communities allowed their people to have Social Security numbers, giving them an easier path to earning a living. For me, it was tough; it was like I had traveled forward in time 200 years.

In the years since I left, I've helped others who've left the Amish community navigate the English world. Many continue working construction for cash because there's no way to immediately get into the system, prove to the government who you are, and then get a job in a factory or anywhere else.

After I received my Social Security number, my boss handed me my first paycheck. I thought, 'Wait a minute. It's not cash anymore. Now it's a check because I have a Social Security number. I'm now part of the taxation system.' I even registered to vote! It felt good. I thought, 'I'm like everybody else—a real grown-up adult!'

After taking a closer look at my paycheck, I asked Blake, "Where's all this money going?"

He explained everything: "This is federal tax, this is social security, this is Medicare, state tax, unemployment tax, and this is the local city tax." He broke it all down.

Shocked, I said, "You've got to be kidding me. I'm keeping only a little more than half of what I earn!"

I started thinking, 'The government is taking a lot of my stuff. How am I supposed to make a living?' That's when I realized the benefit the Amish have with their freedom of religion tax exemption codes. They used to get out of all federal and state taxes and some sales taxes, depending on which community they were in. We were exempt from most taxes, but we paid property tax and school tax, even though we had a private school.

The tax system was hard to accept. I felt like I was being robbed every time I looked at my pay stub. But my friends never acted like it bothered them much and seemed to accept the thievery in stride, and soon I did as well.

35

ENGLISH TECHNOLOGY

I had much to learn in my first days and weeks in the English world. Blake gave me firsthand lessons on how to use the microwave, work a shower, and flush a toilet. Those hands-on lessons were important because I couldn't have figured it out if he had just told me with words. I had no reference point for understanding the explanations of worldly devices, so words meant little. He had to teach me things by showing me step-by-step.

I'm embarrassed to tell you about my first microwave experience. Blake and his family went away somewhere and left me alone at their house to fend for myself and watch television. Blake had shown me how to use the microwave to warm up pizza slices and make popcorn by pressing the buttons with the corresponding pictures. I had been watching wrestling on television, and I was hungry. I grabbed a leftover baked potato and put it in the microwave. Now, please appreciate my ignorance regarding worldly cooking technology. I had been shown how to push the pizza button to heat a slice of pizza and to press the popcorn button to make popcorn. But I had a baked potato, and there was no potato button. So, I reasoned in my mind, 'That button has a pizza, and that button has popcorn. I'd rather have pizza.' I put the potato in the oven and pushed the pizza button. When I opened that microwave, I was incredibly disappointed to find a potato and not a slice of pizza. I thought the world had advanced to the point where it could convert that baked potato into a pizza. At that time, I didn't understand that the buttons were simply timers set for pizza or popcorn. I couldn't wrap my brain around that. I thought if I pushed popcorn, whatever I had in the microwave would turn into popcorn. When he returned, I told Blake about my experience and disappointment, and he laughed hysterically. I was a little insulted because he thought it was so funny. At that moment, Blake realized how he had to show me everything in detail; he couldn't just tell me how something worked.

The washing machine was another hurdle. I'd never encountered such a thing before. I had a concept of how it worked, but the whole notion was foreign to me, so I needed to be shown, step-by-step, how to operate the machine.

Then, there was the shower. Blake showed me how to turn the knob that made the water come on and how to adjust the temperature, and then he walked away. I'm sitting in the tub like we always did when Mom warmed up the water, waiting for the tub to fill. That's what I thought I was supposed to do. He returned and asked from outside the door, "Are you about done yet?"

"Well, I'm just sitting here, waiting for the tub to fill."

He asked, "Do you know you can stand up?"

I didn't know how standing up was going to help. He hadn't followed through by explaining the button to make the water come through the shower head. I was used to sitting down. I didn't feel comfortable standing up and letting the water run over me, like standing outside naked in the rain. All that stuff was new to me. He taught me all the basics. How to flush a toilet and turn on running water— "H is for hot, and C is for cold," He explained. He had to show me all of this. If I didn't know how something worked, I didn't touch it. Whenever I touched something to figure it out, I usually screwed it up. It was quite a battle in the first days and weeks.

36

LIVING ON MY OWN

I am incredibly grateful to Blake and his wife for helping me escape my Amish bondage and for giving me a home; nothing will change my gratitude. But in my desperation to escape my situation and eagerness to obtain freedom, I never stopped to question whether Blake may have a personal motive for helping me. I was so desperate to leave that I probably would have gone to live with anyone who would have taken me in. Maybe I should have stayed with Blake and his family longer than I did, but I wanted to be independent. I wanted to do things myself, and I was starting to see some "red flags" that bothered me.

When I first came to live with Blake and his family, they had asked me to pay half of the rent, which I had no problem doing. Later, I was asked to pay a portion of the electric bill. And after that, the water bill was thrown in. I didn't have a problem with paying any of those expenses because I wanted to do my part. But the increases kept coming to the point where I didn't have any money left to save. I had nothing left over for myself. Initially, I was content just sitting in their living room watching television and eating ice cream because I was free. But after a while, I started thinking about my financial future, and I realized there wasn't much to think about.

I started discussing my concerns about my finances with my buddies at the pallet shop. They started questioning how much I was paying to live with Blake. One of the guys pointed out that my portion of the water bill was more than his entire water bill in the city. Later, I found out that there was no water bill because they lived in the country. Blake and his wife had invented a water bill for me to pay. I didn't realize that they were taking advantage of me, but my friends started showing me things I had no way of knowing. That's when I started paying more attention and began to see things in a new light.

It had been nearly a year when I told Blake that I wanted to move out and get my own place. I expected him to be pleased because I would be out of his house and no longer his responsibility. After all, I had caused him plenty of problems. But he got very upset over my intentions, and I saw something was very familiar to me. When I expressed my desire to move out from under his control, he began to condemn me. He told me that I'd never make it on my own. He said, "I know about the Amish and your background. I know you better than anybody else does. If you trust those other guys and move in with them or get your own apartment, you're not going to make it." I realized he wanted to control me using the same tactics as the Amish used.

I disregarded what he said and moved out of his house. God bless him and his wife for helping me. I love them and respect them for helping me, even if they helped me with selfish motives. I see now what was going on, but I did not understand what I had fallen into at the time.

Some of my other friends at the pallet shop shared a place, so I talked one of them into briefly letting me live with them. But I started drinking in excess, so that didn't last long. They helped me get an apartment, which solved their problem and mine.

I didn't care about the VCR or the television for a while. I just wanted to feel the freedom of having something I was working for that I could call mine. 'This is my apartment...this is my car.' I wanted to have my own stuff.

After wrecking my first car, I had to get a loan for another car—my first loan—and Blake had co-signed for me because I had no credit history. I bought another Plymouth Sundance. This one was much nicer and had lower mileage. I'd been making car payments and paying rent for my apartment. It was government-subsidized housing, where they base rent on your income, but I felt pretty good about myself.

Everyone who walked into my apartment back then was surprised by my minimalistic surroundings. They probably wondered if I had truly left the Amish. I didn't want any more bills, so I didn't have anything. I was just happy and content sitting alone in silence, drinking beer and savoring freedom—no religious ties. I felt free. Nobody with a long beard and a hat was going to roll up in a horse and buggy and tell me, "You messed up again," or get after my dad about me riding a bicycle. I could relax and read books. I had a flush toilet inside my apartment. I remember how amazing it was to flush my own toilet—that was a big deal.

By the time I moved to my own place, I'd mastered most of the worldly technology. I eventually got a TV and a VCR, and I started renting and watching movies. That was a huge accomplishment, I thought.

Once I was living on my own, I told my buddies at the pallet shop, "I'd like to find me a girl." One of the guys introduced me to his sister-in-law, Elizabeth. At the time, I didn't know that he didn't like his sister-in-law very much. In hindsight, that knowledge might have saved me some misery and a bunch of money. I started dating Elizabeth, who turned out to be a great cook, and I dearly missed good food.

My world soon revolved around staying up late at night watching movies, working at the pallet shop, my new girl, and her cooking. When I first brought Elizabeth to my apartment, she asked in amazement, "This is all you have? There's not much in here. You have no pictures on the walls, no decorations."

I explained to her, "I don't need those things, and I don't have any pictures to put on the wall." It looked like an Amish house with bare walls. I knew I needed a woman to straighten that out for me. I needed many things straightened out, things way beyond my décor.

One of the dangers I faced in living alone was breaking the law without realizing I was doing it. And while I had grown up in a legalistic environment, the punishments were relatively inconsequential unless you crossed the line to eternal damnation. That was not true of breaking the rules in the English world. I should have submitted to a mentor for a longer period. But I was bullheaded, and knowing what you don't know is impossible. My stubbornness soon demanded a heavy payment.

37

DUI AND ALCOHOL

I t's common for young people who leave the Amish to run amok with worldly things; I was no exception. Like many, I went to parties, bars, clubs—nudie clubs. Because I started hanging around people who shared that lifestyle, it was easy to start doing all the other things they did because they accepted and loved me—or so it seemed. Really, people who live sinful lives mostly want other people to join them and validate their choices. Since I didn't understand love, I fell for this deception.

All this self-gratifying behavior is called 'fun.' In the back of my mind, I was still thinking that I needed to have as much fun as possible, find peace within myself, be happy, and live how I wanted before facing my inevitable damnation.

Eventually, I was stopped by the police and arrested for DUI one night. For those of you too innocent to know, that means I was Driving Under the Influence of some substance that impaired my ability to drive. I drank alcohol to excess and drove quite often, and my buddies did the same thing. It was extremely common, and I might add, very dangerous and stupid. Sometimes, I used marijuana and even crack cocaine. That night, vodka was my chosen companion. I was introduced to stuff that could have easily destroyed my life or caused me to destroy someone else's life.

I was driving home after a night of drinking, and my tire went flat. I didn't realize my tire was flat because I had a good buzz and was oblivious to the cares of life, which included the condition of my rear tire. I passed a state trooper who couldn't help but notice sparks flying in the air from a rear tire that had long since shredded and left the rim.

After lighting me up, I managed to get the car off the road and stop. The state trooper approached my car with obvious concern, well aware that anyone driving so obliviously was likely not thinking clearly and could be dangerous. Prepared for any scenario, he cautiously made his way toward my vehicle.

In a move that was utterly stupid and risky, I reached into the back seat and retrieved my nearly empty bottle of vodka. Remarkably, the trooper didn't shoot me. In a staggering display of drunken poor judgment and in a ridiculous attempt to be sociable, I offered him a drink. He politely declined and commented, "No, I will not have any of that with you. But did you know you have a flat tire?"

I responded, somewhat bewildered, "No, I hadn't noticed."

In a straightforward tone, he instructed, "Well, come back here and take a look at it."

Upon exiting the car, I immediately fell face-first onto the road. The trooper, with a touch of dry humor, asked, "Have you had a little to drink?"

Picking myself up from the road, I replied with equal parts honesty and sarcasm, "Nope, I've had a lot to drink. Didn't you see that bottle? It's almost empty!"

He instructed, "Blow into this device." I complied.

At that moment, I didn't attempt to evade responsibility or conceal my guilt. The reality was clear: I was caught, and I knew I was going to jail. I desired to inject as much humor into the situation as I could, trying to make the trooper laugh. Surprisingly, he didn't handcuff me or treat me with any harshness. In fact, we ended up sharing a few laughs together. He admitted later, "I've never laughed so much while arresting someone for DUI in my entire career as a police officer." Throughout the incident, I offered no resistance and caused no trouble.

As we rode together in the police car, our conversation turned to my Amish background. We joked and laughed on our way to the jail, where I was eventually booked. After my three-day stay in jail and subsequent DUI conviction, my license was suspended. That's when I seriously began to contemplate the direction my life had taken.

For nineteen years since leaving the Amish, I lived a life that consisted of going to clubs and bars, partying, and drinking. This path is not uncommon among those who have experienced mental, emotional, and physical abuse, especially within highly controlled religious environments. Such environments often foster feelings of hopelessness and entrapment. This period of my life was filled with risks that could have easily ended my life prematurely. But God was watching over me, and I am still here today by His grace and mercy.

38

WOMEN AND FAILED RELATIONSHIPS

S hortly after meeting Elizabeth, I invited her to my apartment and straight up asked her if she wanted to get married. In my upbringing, marriage was more pragmatic than romantic. Growing up in a closed community meant that young men and women had similar expectations of marriage since we shared a well-defined and mutually understood culture. That's not the case in the English world, where the culture is far more diverse. I didn't grasp this reality at the time.

Asking Elizabeth to marry me felt like the right thing to do. It was the next logical step to getting what I wanted, which was mostly food and sex. She looked at me in bewilderment when I asked her. She even talked to her father about it. Her whole family seemed perplexed and didn't understand why I wanted to marry their daughter so soon. I have no idea why they didn't talk her out of it.

I thought marrying a woman would please God. I thought pleasing God might help my cause, and marriage came with sex and food, so it seemed like a good idea at the time. Sex is for marriage, so kissing and touching were off-limits. However, driven by mutual consent and my own impatience, we ended up crossing some of those boundaries prematurely. But I wanted to ensure we got married quickly, and we did. And so began what would become the first of many failed relationships.

Our marriage—if you can call it that—was short-lived. The cultural gap between us was wide: she struggled to understand my Amish background, and honestly, I was equally perplexed by her English ways. What she didn't realize was the extent of what I needed to learn. She wanted a partner who was a natural leader; I was searching for someone to guide me, to teach me the things I didn't know. Our needs and expectations were totally misaligned, and far from "equally yoked."

Financially, we were on different pages too. She loved to spend money on material things like jewelry and various luxuries. On the other hand, I was inclined to save. Having owned very little in my life, the idea of an English woman spending all my hard-earned money was unnerving to me. My goal was to build a life, to make something meaningful out of my existence, without the burden of an uncontrolled spender holding me back. It became clear that our paths and priorities were totally incompatible.

I was broke throughout my entire relationship with Elizabeth. My financial situation was horrible; I had nothing to spare. Her desires for stuff seemed endless. She always wanted to shop at the mall, always wanting something. I remember thinking to myself, 'Amish women certainly don't spend money like this.' When I ran out of money, she wanted credit cards to buy more stuff. The debt accumulated during our time together became so insufferable it became financially impossible for me to continue in the relationship.

We both needed to learn how to show affection. Elizabeth often felt as though I despised her. Despite the many relationships I've had since then, her words still echo painfully in my mind: "Why do you hate me?"

Confused by her question, I asked, "Why would you say that?" After all, I didn't harbor any hatred toward her.

Her reply revealed the core of my shortcomings: "You never say 'I love you.' You don't show any affection."

She genuinely believed I hated her, and reflecting on it now, I can see her perspective. What I failed to communicate to her, because I couldn't, was that affection was a foreign concept in my upbringing. In my family home, I witnessed the opposite of affection. I never heard my parents exchange words of love, nor did I see them embrace or kiss. These expressions of love were lessons I still needed to learn. Elizabeth was not prepared to teach me how to show affection or to guide me in expressing love verbally or physically.

In hindsight, her feelings were valid. It's reasonable for a spouse to expect expressions of love and affection. But at that time, I was simply incapable of meeting those expectations.

Our relationship was doomed from the start by my own ignorance. When I first asked Elizabeth if she wanted to get married, my approach left her surprised. It was a far cry from what she expected out of a marriage proposal. In the English world, proposals typically involve a certain romantic ritual—getting down on one knee and presenting a ring. But I never heard of these customs; I didn't even fully grasp what it meant to "propose." So, when I asked her about getting married, I unknowingly violated all the normal things she expected.

It never occurred to me to find out what she wanted from a marriage. In retrospect, I realize my insensitivity and ignorance contributed to the confusion and disconnect in our relationship.

Elizabeth's parents had a long conversation with me about the proper way to propose. They explained, "You're supposed to ask us for permission and get a ring." I respectfully followed their advice despite it being foreign to me, and it ended up costing me $2,000. I had to take out a loan for the ring and other expenses. Throughout the whole process, I was thinking, 'Why would you go broke buying jewelry for just one finger?' In my mind, the Amish way seemed so much more practical and cost-effective. Amish men simply grow a beard to signify marriage, and women change their cap color from black to white. No extravagant expenditures. Why was a ring necessary?

Despite my reservations, I understood that these customs were part of entering into the English world—a world I had now chosen over my Amish roots. If the entrance fee was a $2,000 ring, then I was prepared to pay it, even if it meant going into debt. I was committed to doing things correctly. I followed through with the entire ritual, including getting down on one knee, as expected.

The wedding ceremony was a surreal experience. There was a rehearsal where I was instructed on every detail—what to do, where to stand, what to say. I felt like an animal being trained by its handlers. The entire strange and unfamiliar ritual seemed to symbolize what my life was becoming: a series of learned behaviors that were foreign to my nature and seemed to serve no discernible purpose.

Given the brevity of our marriage, a formal divorce wasn't necessary. We simply agreed on the division of our belongings and parted ways, although we remained friends.

I abandoned the notion of marriage; I just threw out the idea—I didn't care anymore. I numbed my guilt by going to bars where I picked up different women every weekend. I just lived how I wanted while avoiding serious relationships.

I suppose I wanted relationships, but I didn't want what the relationships brought or demanded, if that makes any sense. The experience with Elizabeth had a dramatic effect on my outlook. I wanted to be happy, free of religion, free of the control of women who spent my money, all that kind of stuff. I went through many years of one failed relationship after another. Most of the failures surrounded my lack of affection, a singular affliction that seemed destined to block my path to happiness.

39

TENSION AT THE PALLET SHOP

After leaving Blake's home and transitioning into my apartment, tension set in at the pallet shop. Blake began treating me harshly for reasons I didn't fully understand at the time. Things became so tense that I couldn't take it anymore; I needed to find another job.

I didn't want to confront Blake, so I returned to work one evening after everybody else went home. I knew the owner always stayed late to do paperwork. I told him that I couldn't work there any longer. I didn't go into details because I knew he respected Blake. It was a very uncomfortable situation. The owner always bragged about my Amish work ethic, how I stayed at my job and didn't take smoke breaks—as was the habit of many. I had no problem working through my lunch if needed. I just kept going and going and going. I told him that I had bigger dreams and goals, and I was moving on.

I turned in my uniform shirt and name tag. They were precious to me because they made me feel like I belonged to something I had chosen. But now it was time to walk away. It was painful but necessary.

Elizabeth had worked as an automotive contractor for Honda, Toyota, and Ford. She told me, "I'll talk to them. You can probably get a job there." She talked to her supervisor, and I got a job sorting parts. I developed a different perspective of the world from working with a far more diverse group of people. I worked on an assembly line, inspecting parts for defects before they went on a car.

I was amazed at how worldly cars were assembled. It was incredible to watch the assembly process, with each person putting their part on the car as it moved along the line. I never regretted leaving the pallet shop. The technology I witnessed was light-years from the pallet shop—it was an entirely different world. They used robotic arms to attach parts and weld metal with incredible precision and consistency. I found the whole process fascinating.

One day in August 2006, I was sitting in the Honda plant break room eating my lunch. People often brought newspapers into the break room and would leave them there for others to read. I casually glanced at a newspaper on the table and saw an article titled "Couple Sentenced to Prison Terms for Shoplifting." What really caught my attention was the second paragraph, which contained the names of Blake and his wife. I continued reading the article: "A couple was sentenced to four years in prison for using their three teenage daughters to help them shoplift thousands of dollars' worth of merchandise to be resold on the Internet." My first thought was, 'No way. That can't be them. They're the ones who helped me leave the Amish. They're loving people. They wouldn't do that to their kids.'

The article went on to state that they had been convicted two months prior for a pattern of corrupt activity and child endangerment, having used their minor daughters to steal more than $56,000 in merchandise from stores in multiple counties and then storing it at their farmhouse for sale on eBay. Their oldest daughter and youngest son were living with their grandmother, and the other two girls were in foster care.

I was so shocked by what I had just read that I could hardly move. I didn't want to believe it, but the facts were all there. I had trusted these people and couldn't imagine that they were capable of this type of deception or of using their children in this manner.

It took me quite a while to come to grips with this reality. Later, I spoke with their oldest daughter, who had by this time turned eighteen, and she confirmed everything. She also added some details, which were even more chilling. This is also a good time to tell you that Blake is not his real name. I have intentionally withheld real names to protect the family, especially the children.

After reading the article and later talking to the oldest daughter, I couldn't help but feel that God had protected me throughout my time spent living with Blake. I didn't know God then. I didn't read the Bible. But, looking back, I praise God for His divine protection because I could have easily been sucked into their scheme, just like their children.

Their daughter confirmed that things started about the time I lived there. Now I understand why Blake was so upset by my leaving. Many of the other things I saw at that time now make sense. Their daughter expressed to me that her parents' behavior changed after I moved out and that they were desperate for money. They started having their daughters steal items from stores, and they made a business out of it. About two and a half years after I moved out of Blake's home, their behavior got even worse. According to their daughters, it got to the point where they felt physically threatened to continue stealing for their parents.

I don't know their intentions for me, but I have a feeling they planned to suck me into it their scheme. When I moved out unexpectedly—praise God for protecting me—they used their children, their own flesh and blood. If they could do it to their own kids, then certainly they could do it to a naïve and scared former Amish.

I've never spoken with Blake and his wife since being sentenced to prison. I knew there was no reason to ask them if they were guilty. I never felt led to reach out to them. I was just blessed that the Lord saved me from what could have been a very horrible situation. It dawned on me that if I had stayed with Blake any longer—instead of sorting parts at a Honda plant—I'd have been headed to prison for four years just like they were. I was over eighteen when I lived with them and considered an adult in the eyes of the law. If I had fallen into their trap, I would have been charged as an adult and done prison time.

You never know what is going on inside a person. I don't think this was on Blake's mind when he agreed to help me years prior and told me to wait until I was eighteen. I believe he genuinely cared and wanted to help me. I'll never know what happened in Blake's life that led him to justify such a horrible thing against his own children. In writing this, I don't want to bring them further shame or condemnation—that's not my place. They have since been released from prison and released from probation. They have a huge debt to pay. I hope they somehow reconcile with their children and seek forgiveness for everyone's sake. But more than anything, I hope they find peace and freedom in Jesus Christ.

The one lesson I learned through this is to recognize and respect when the feeling comes to move on. It's important to pay attention to those signals.

40

MEETING NIKKI

Several years after I left my Amish home, my twin brother, Levi, started thinking of leaving. But his situation was complicated by a girl, Naomi. He married Naomi and relocated to a different Amish community in Huntingdon, Tennessee. When I learned of this, I was eager to visit them at their new home. Every year since, Levi and I celebrated our birthday together. This is a tradition we've kept, although the celebration looks a bit different now.

Levi and Naomi had become part of a more liberal Amish community, one that wasn't overly concerned with my status as a former Amish. My brother and I partied in the basement of their home. Equipped with boom boxes and radios, we included other Amish who were eager to join in. For Levi and me, it was like experiencing our own version of Rumspringa—a period of exploration traditionally granted to Amish youth—which we never had in our Old-Order Amish upbringing.

These events were an eye-opener for me. I saw Amish teenagers putting down beer after beer, something that would have been unthinkable in our original community. This Amish group allowed worldly-issued IDs. Those of age could legally purchase alcohol, or they would have their drivers—local non-Amish neighbors—buy it for them. We had some great parties with kegs and cases of beer and lots of people.

I recall that sometime around 2002, I was celebrating our birthday at Levi's place and noticed him and some of our cousins giggling over a cell phone—they weren't technically allowed to have cell phones, but they did anyway. They were laughing and joking with someone over the phone. After a night of drinking and partying, I had a good buzz, and my curiosity got the better of me. I asked, "Who are you guys talking to?"

They responded nonchalantly, "Oh, it's someone from back home, near where you live in Ohio."

Intrigued, I asked, "Can I speak with this person?" That was the first time I heard the voice of Nikki, who would later become my wife. It was an unexpected turn of events: here I was, a former Amish for about five years, connecting with my future spouse through my still-Amish twin brother. Levi and my cousins had been involved in construction projects for Nikki's parents, which had kept them in touch. They were chatting long-distance from Tennessee back to Ohio.

True to my ever-present hunt for food, as soon as I joined the call, in true Eli-fashion, I casually asked Nikki, "When I get back home, can I come over for dinner?" She agreed. I didn't know it then, but that moment changed my life.

When I returned home Nikki welcomed me with a spaghetti dinner. I returned again and again, like a starving stray dog, drawn not only to the delicious food but also by Nikki herself. It took a while before we officially started dating; my visits were initially motivated by the meals she prepared. But as time went on, my affection for Nikki grew. We spent many hours simply talking and sharing meals with her family, and we frequently engaged in long phone conversations. Eventually, I asked her out on a proper date.

When the time felt right, I decided to propose to her in the traditional manner I had learned. I asked her parents' blessing, got down on one knee, and asked her to marry me in what I believed to be the "right" way. To my joy, she said "yes"!

This was how I met Nikki Yoder—through my Amish brother and cousins, who were enjoying their own kind of freedom in their community in Tennessee. Marrying Nikki turned out to be the best decision of my life.

41

NO TURNING BACK

Nikki was amazing. She went with me to visit my father at his farm. Unlike my mother, my father wasn't concerned about me coming beyond the curve of the driveway; he was always open to seeing me. When he met Nikki, he immediately recognized her. He knew her parents from their business dealings over the years and recognized her immediately. In making the connection, a broad smile of approval spread across my father's face. Realizing that my father recognized and approved of my wife was a heartwarming moment.

Their interaction was a joy to witness. They exchanged smiles, laughter, and jokes, and his acceptance of her was amazing. It was beautiful to see such warmth in their exchanges. The three of us visited several places together, spending precious time and creating memories. Having this time with my father was a blessing, especially with Nikki by my side.

Nikki and I continued our visits for over a year. She became an important part of my efforts to support my father. Persistent depression and alcohol addiction took a heavy toll on him. He would share his latest grievances about being shunned by the Amish community each time we visited. One incident he recounted involved him driving a tractor, an act that led to his shunning by the community.

My father suffered a back injury serious enough to require surgery while helping with a barn-raising. His back pain was so severe that it kept him home from church, which provided Nikki and me the opportunity to visit him more frequently. These visits were special to me, as they gave us the chance to form a deeper relationship.

During one of these visits, he expressed his longing for the kind of freedom I found outside the Amish community. I remember thinking skeptically, 'He won't leave because he's got a large family.' I recalled an attempt he made to leave the community when I was a child. He had cut off all his hair, including his beard, and adopted an English appearance. Despite this drastic change, he never fully left and eventually went back to his Amish lifestyle. He grew his hair back and eventually rejoined the church.

As our visits continued and his declarations about leaving became more earnest, I started to take his intentions seriously. We saw him every other Sunday, and during one of these visits, he firmly stated his wish to leave. He even set a specific date and time to leave.

Nikki and I were thrilled at the prospect. Anticipating his needs in this new chapter of his life, we decided to search for a larger, more suitable vehicle so we could all travel together comfortably. We understood that we'd eventually need to teach him how to drive and assist him in obtaining a driver's license—all the things I'd needed to get. I was determined to ensure his transition was smoother than mine had been. Preparing to help Henry Yoder become a free man was a thrilling undertaking. In a way, it was like expecting a newborn child! I was excited for him to discover freedom as I had.

Along with my excitement over my father's impending freedom, I had significant concerns about his alcoholism and depression. But my anticipation and excitement over a real relationship with him overshadowed my worries. I reassured him, "Okay, Dad, we will be there at 9:00 a.m. on Sunday."

I was at a car dealership in preparation for my dad's escape when I received a panicked call from my brother, Levi, in Tennessee. He was crying uncontrollably over the phone. It took him a moment to compose himself enough to relay the shocking news: Dad had attempted suicide. The family had heard a gunshot and had found him behind the barn, still alive but critically injured from a gunshot to his head. The turmoil was overheard by English neighbors, who called 911. A helicopter was dispatched to the scene to airlift him to a hospital in Lima, Ohio.

Levi had received the shocking news from an English neighbor just minutes before calling me. Coincidentally, I was in Lima, Ohio, finalizing a car purchase near St. Rita's Medical Center. I saw the helicopter heading toward the hospital and knew he was on board. The car salesman was taken aback when Nikki and I abruptly ran out of his office. Despite feeling bad about our hasty departure, we rushed to the hospital without hesitation.

Upon arriving, I approached the receptionist and explained, "My Amish father is here, and I need to see him." Nikki and I were quickly ushered to a waiting area. Soon, a doctor approached us. Looking me over, he asked, "You're his son? He's an Amish man."

I confirmed, "Yes, I'm a former Amish. That really is my father." To prove my identity, I presented my driver's license showing Eli Yoder. The doctor accepted it without question and promptly handed me some paperwork to sign.

"He's in serious condition," the doctor informed me, "but there's a slim chance we can save him. We need to perform surgery immediately on his head. Your signature is required for the release."

I consented without hesitation, "I'll sign it right now." In my mind, I thought this might be the only opportunity to save his life. Signing the document felt like a great honor. With my signature in place, the surgery began immediately.

As my father underwent surgery, Nikki and I were directed to a waiting area near the intensive care unit. We settled in and braced ourselves for the uncertainty of the hours ahead. Before long, my Amish relatives started trickling in; their arrival was delayed due to their dependence on drivers. Among them was my mother.

Her first concern was to question my decision: "You signed up for brain surgery? We don't do that," she said with evident disapproval. I replied firmly, "I'm trying to save his life." But what followed was even more unnerving. Her attention shifted from my father's critical condition to my attire. Despite the gravity of the situation, she fixated on the fact that I wasn't wearing traditional Amish clothing. At the farm, she had always insisted on this, but I hadn't expected it to be a concern at the hospital. I was mistaken. She claimed she couldn't bear to look at me.

As more Amish family members arrived, she addressed me publicly, insisting, "Eli, you're going to have to change. You cannot look worldly like that."

I was devastated. While dealing with my father's life-threatening situation, my mother's primary concern was my appearance. I struggled to comprehend her priorities, but then again, it wasn't entirely surprising. After all, she was the daughter of Bishop Levi Beachy.

Nikki suggested a compromise: "Let's go to the local Goodwill store and try to appease her somewhat. Maybe a pair of black pants and a white shirt, something close to their Sunday best—black and white." That's exactly what we did. At Goodwill, we found a plain white shirt, though it had a lay-down collar, which I knew would be an issue. The cuff on the front was more than three inches, another issue for sure. And without suspenders, the outfit was still far from meeting the strict standards of official Amish attire.

Nevertheless, I did what I could. All decked out in my new black pants and a white shirt buttoned up to the neck, we returned to the hospital. My shoes were still not in compliance, but there was little we could do about that. My mother's reaction was mixed. "Well, at least you made an effort. That's better." However, she couldn't hide her distress over the lay-down collar. A lay-down collar was very worldly, and God wouldn't allow anybody into Heaven—she believed—with a lay-down collar. At this point, considering all my other indiscretions, you'd think the collar wouldn't even be noticed.

Being somewhat in compliance with the dress code allowed Nikki and I to be part of the family gathering at the hospital. The waiting area was bustling with what seemed like hundreds of relatives—cousins, aunts, uncles—owing to the sheer size of our family. The interactions varied. Some approached me, offering handshakes and brief expressions of concern. Others chose to ignore my presence entirely, not even acknowledging that I was there. The air was thick with tension, though not necessarily for the reasons a casual observer might assume.

Some of my Amish relatives attempted conversation, but their words were colored with judgment. "Oh, is this your girlfriend? I guess you won't be returning if you've found someone new," one commented. Another remarked, "We heard about your previous marriage. Now with another woman, huh? That kind of behavior will send you to Hell." Their comments were rife with rudeness and passive-aggression.

There I was, with my father's life hanging in the balance, and these family members seemed more preoccupied with flaunting their pompous, fabricated virtue and pointing out my perceived moral failings. Their deplorable, brazen display of disdain sickened me.

The events at the hospital gave Nikki a first-hand understanding of my background and the complexities of my Amish family. The contrast between their usual conduct and their behavior during a crisis showcased their bizarre priorities. Strangely enough, this entire ordeal brought Nikki and me even closer together. Until then, her exposure to the Amish had been limited to their commendable work ethic and craftsmanship. This encounter revealed the legalistic side of the community that valued church rules over human decency and compassion.

Nikki was deeply affected by what she witnessed that day. Nikki remained by my side throughout that tumultuous ordeal. I remain unspeakably grateful for her unwavering support, her comforting presence, and our shared tears during such a difficult time.

Following the surgery, my father was placed on a ventilator—a life support system. A meeting between the elders and the bishop of the church was held, and their decision promptly declared: "We must remove that worldly machine. It's imperative to trust in God and not rely on a computer—it's the mark of the beast." To some of them, the life-support machine, critical for my father's survival post-surgery, was seen as part of the "beast system." They were referring to the Book of Revelation in the Bible, where the "beast" is a symbol in a prophetic vision representing anti-Christian powers or authorities.

This decision sparked considerable controversy as evening approached on the second day. While the church authorities were adamant about disconnecting the ventilator, the doctor, who remained hopeful for my father's recovery, argued against it. Among the church members and family present, some agreed with the church's stance, while others believed in the doctor's judgment, stating, "If the doctor believes it's beneficial, perhaps he'll pull through."

The doctor, bound by his professional principles, suggested, "There's always a chance," even though, deep down, I believe he knew the likelihood was slim. The church members remained troubled by the life-support machine. As tensions rose, my twin brother approached the doctor with a direct request for honesty: "Is there any real chance for Dad, or is it certain he'll pass if we turn off the machine?"

After a brief pause, the doctor met my brother's gaze. "You want the truth? I'll give it to you," he said, his tone somber. "Your father is already brain-dead." The news was met with a collective gasp throughout the room.

"You're saying he's only alive because of that machine?" was the incredulous response from the family.

The doctor confirmed, "If you're seeking the truth, then yes. If we remove the life support, he will pass within ten minutes."

At that moment, the grim reality set in. The entire Amish family, huddled in the hospital lobby, now understood that turning off the machine would mean the inevitable. Despite their faith, the harsh truth was that my father was already beyond the point of recovery. The lobby, crowded with over a hundred Amish relatives, fell into silence so deep you could have heard a feather drop.

After a long and heavy pause, a consensus was reached: "Turn it off."

As they prepared to disconnect the life-support machine, only immediate family members were allowed into my father's room. I could feel my mother's gaze on me, heavy with unspoken words. Eventually, she came closer and whispered in my ear, "Don't you want to take your dad's hand and apologize for leaving the Amish?"

I was taken aback by her suggestion and simply replied, "No."

Tears filled her eyes as she pleaded, "Why wouldn't you want to make things right? He might still be able to hear you."

My response was firm: "Mom, whether he can hear me or not, I have nothing to reconcile with him."

She persisted, "But you left the Amish. You didn't honor your father and your mother."

I didn't waver, "No, Mom. No." Inside, I wrestled with a heavy secret—I was meant to pick up Dad that day; he was planning to leave the Amish. But she didn't know that, and I chose not to tell her.

The room was filled with the sounds of my family's muffled sobbing—my brothers, sisters, and those immediately related to us. And then, they turned off the life support. The monitor's line flattened immediately, signaling the end. Henry Yoder was gone.

My participation in my father's funeral was conditional: I could attend if I wore traditional Amish attire and concealed my worldly hairstyle. On the day of the funeral, I rode in a buggy with my family, holding my little brother, Melvin, on my lap. Melvin was very young when I left the Amish. We barely knew each other, but his presence provided a bit of solace in that moment. As we made our way to the graveyard, Nikki and my cousin followed at a respectful distance in their car—a symbol of our worldly life that was met with disapproval by the Amish community. Two of my cousins who had also left the Amish community showed remarkable kindness and support. They put on their Amish clothes and accompanied me.

My father was denied a traditional Amish funeral. The community viewed his suicide as equivalent to murder and limited attendees to family members, some church members, and the elders.

I was allowed to stand up front with the family at the grave site. I sensed their gaze fixed on me, scrutinizing my every reaction. I imagine they wondered if I would break down, regret leaving the Amish, or show some sign of remorse. Amid these thoughts, I chose to stand tall and hold my head high while meeting their stares without a flinch. I didn't shed a tear. I stood aloof with my arms folded while others wept around the casket. I did not give in to their expectations. I observed the burial rituals with a sense of detachment as they performed their customary acts—placing boards atop the casket before it was buried. Although I was physically present, I felt emotionally distant from the surrounding people.

When the ceremony concluded, I departed quietly, choosing not to engage further with my family. I joined Nikki and my cousin in the car, and we left.

In the aftermath of the funeral, the Amish church erected a fence around my father's grave, isolating him in a corner of the cemetery. This physical separation symbolized the community's judgment. The Amish church had initially proposed to my mother that my father be buried outside the Amish cemetery without any marker or identification, as they deemed him unworthy to rest among the "holy."

I later learned my mother was deeply upset by this suggestion and voiced her disagreement. The church conceded to burying him within the cemetery but insisted on the fence. In doing so, they marked his final resting place as a "dirty grave"—that of a condemned individual. This differentiation from other graves was a painful reminder of the community's condemnation and a stinging indictment against my grieving family.

I started drinking heavily and more often at that time. I regularly visited the cemetery, and often drank an entire case of beer by my father's grave. The alcohol barely numbed the depth of my despair, which spiraled into suicidal thoughts. I grappled with the same dark contemplations that had consumed my father despite not fully comprehending his reasons. His actions left me with countless unanswered questions.

One night, my friends and I, fueled by alcohol and emotion, decided to make a statement at the cemetery. We tore down the fence surrounding my father's grave in defiance of what it represented. The Amish church responded by building a sturdier fence reinforced with metal posts. My friends and I returned in defiance for another gathering at the cemetery, ripped out this new metal fence, and threw it into the creek to watch it drift away.

After our destruction of the second fence, the Amish church stopped their efforts to isolate my father's grave. It became clear to them that I was resolute in my refusal to abide by their rules and judgments. I didn't have to submit to their church and their self-imposed rules—their cult. Dismantling the fence wasn't so much about rebelling against their authority as it was about upholding my father's dignity in the only way I knew how.

When I visited my father's grave, I often left flowers as a token of my affection and respect. The Amish community burned the flowers I placed there. I was aware that the Amish do not traditionally decorate graves, but their harshness felt like an extension of the condemnation they had already heaped upon my father and me by extension. It was a cruel irony that even in death, the condemned were denied a simple gesture of comfort.

This destruction persisted for several years. I eventually resorted to setting up hidden cameras near the grave to capture evidence of those responsible for the continuous vandalism and violation of my father's final resting place.

I learned later from my uncle that the Amish church had gathered at the cemetery to read an excommunication letter over my father's grave. It is customary among the Old-Order Amish to read an official excommunication letter to anyone who has been shunned or excommunicated. If a person just picks up and leaves, they send the letter to that person. This was done for anyone not forgiven by the church through a vote. This letter was more than a separation from the community; it was an official condemnation of a person's soul. They had not voted to forgive my father, so they chose to read the letter over his grave as their final judgment.

My father's suicide was a crushing blow. He took his life the day before he was going to leave, a decision he had come to on his own. I was so excited for my father to have a taste of liberty and freedom, to escape the oppression that had defined his entire life.

The reason behind his decision to take his own life remains a mystery to me—a question that echoes in the silence left by his absence. It's an ugly reminder of the powerful influence and control that a destructive, cult-like environment can wield over an individual. My father's life, marred by years of humiliation and dehumanizing treatment, compounded by his struggles with depression and alcoholism, ended in a senseless tragedy.

42

FATHERHOOD

Three years after the tragedy of my father's suicide, a significant event occurred in my life—the birth of my son. The arrival of a man's first child is often viewed as a rite of passage where a son becomes a father. It's an event filled with excitement, hope, and promise, marking a new chapter filled with endless possibilities for the future.

Following my father's suicide, I plunged into a deep depression and engaged in self-destructive behaviors that threatened my physical, mental, and spiritual well-being. My life was dominated by a reckless disregard for my health and an endless pursuit of drugs, alcohol, and pornography, each acting as an agent for further self-destruction. My efforts to escape my pain were compounding my problems and feeding my destructive behavior. My conduct toward my wife, who needed my support more than ever, was far from what it should have been. Instead of offering her the care and understanding she deserved, she was met with my scorn.

The arrival of our child triggered a complex mixture of emotions. While the prospect of fatherhood filled me with excitement, I also questioned whether the child she carried belonged to me. My behavior was deplorable; it's a powerful testimony of how alcohol, drugs, and sin in general, can cause a person to destroy their own life and that of those they hold dear. It is a regrettable part of my past.

Cutting the umbilical cord in the hospital snapped me into a new reality—I was now a father. The birth of my son was an exhilarating experience. Despite my excitement, I was ill-prepared for the myriad responsibilities that fatherhood required. In the Amish community, men typically focused on farm work while women cared for the children. My upbringing did nothing to prepare me for the hands-on aspects of parenting. Changing diapers and managing nighttime feedings was a new and overwhelming challenge. It was a difficult adjustment, but I committed myself to meeting the demands of parenthood, although I had several missteps along the way.

My behavior during this time was heavily influenced by the shadow of my father's alcoholism, which I inadvertently mirrored. Despite my strong desire to avoid becoming the person I had always criticized, I found myself trapped in a cycle of self-destructive behavior that seemed inescapable. The joys and responsibilities of fatherhood, as life-altering as they were, did not motivate me to overcome these habits.

Thinking back on this time, I feel intense shame for not seizing the opportunity to make significant changes in my life; it's a painful part of my past.

43

GED AND CDL

The Amish eighth grade was my highest level of education, which included reading, writing, history, math, some geography, and German. My education served the purposes of the Amish lifestyle, but it fell short of a high school diploma or a GED equivalent. Getting a job without a high school diploma or GED was challenging, to say the least.

Neither the pallet shop nor the inspection job required a GED for employment. I appreciated my previous work experience, but these opportunities stressed the limitations I faced regarding job availability and my potential for earning money. I possessed skills and knowledge vital to life in the Amish community, but I held little value in the broader job market. I needed to upgrade my skills if I was going to do anything beyond physical labor.

In 2008, the United States was hit by a significant recession. This economic downturn drastically affected the automotive industry, leading major manufacturers like Honda, Ford, GM, Toyota, and Nissan to terminate employees hired through temporary employment services and contractors. I was among those who found themselves abruptly cut from employment. The recession made finding a job extremely difficult, and my lack of a GED became a solid barrier. Despite completing numerous applications, I never received a single response. I was simply unemployable.

It dawned on me that this might be an opportune moment to reassess my options. Perhaps it was time to close some old doors, look for new beginnings, and reach for growth and advancement that had previously seemed out of reach.

I visited the local job and family services center, known as One Stop. I posed a straightforward question: "I've been recently laid off and currently rely on unemployment; what high-demand job can I train for?" The options presented were quite diverse. The roles spanned from police officer, firefighter, paramedic, and nurse's aide, among other service-oriented positions. However, truck driving was mentioned as being in particularly high demand.

The idea of driving a truck was both intriguing and intimidating. I wasn't sure I could drive a truck. Most of my driving experience involved horses, and my history with automobiles was not the best, but I thought it was worth a shot. The conversation took a familiar turn when they inquired about my educational background: "Do you have a GED or a high school diploma?"

My response was a resigned "No."

Their advice was direct and practical: "Since you're currently on unemployment, it might be a good idea to obtain your GED first, then pursue a CDL (Commercial Driver's License)." That advice revealed a path I hadn't considered, and I followed their advice to the letter.

There were several available options for GED classes. I attended daily classes where I learned writing and algebra—a concept entirely foreign to me at the time. Exploring new academic territories was eye-opening. I even adapted to using a calculator for certain math problems. After attending GED classes for six months, the teacher said, "I think you need at least a year."

I had already set my sights on obtaining my CDL and beginning a career in truck driving, despite my teacher's reservations about my readiness. "Let me take the test, anyway," I stated. They wanted me to write an essay because that was one of the last things I had to learn before taking the test. They put an essay exam before me, and I failed miserably. They said my writing was a mess. I still said, "I want to take the test to see where I'm at. Maybe I'll surprise you guys and pass it."

My Amish heritage instilled a stubbornness that has acted as both a blessing and a curse throughout my life. Tenacity is a deeply ingrained part of my character. The skepticism from my GED instructors about my readiness for the exam only hardened my resolve.

They relented and allowed me to take the exam. To everyone's surprise, and perhaps my own, I passed on my first attempt. The algebra section was where I did the best. My essay left much to be desired. But my strong performance in math and other sections compensated for my lackluster writing skills, and I passed the GED exam.

I wasted no time. I applied for truck driver schooling within two weeks of obtaining my GED. The 2008 recession was so bad, I was given a $5,000 grant to attend CDL School. That covered me for a six-week program. It included the classroom and the actual driving lessons, where I learned to drive a Freightliner semi-truck with a ten-speed manual transmission. I drove at night, learned to back a trailer, and how to hit the dock just right. There are lots of rules to learn about driving a truck and lots of safety procedures. I learned them all.

I made a point to be in class early every morning for both my GED and CDL training, without missing a single day. To me, this wasn't anything out of the ordinary. I had a clear picture of what I wanted and the steps necessary to achieve it, so I followed through. What did surprise me was the lack of commitment from others in the classes. Many of my classmates struggled to get out of bed and show up consistently.

My CDL teacher, Sam Wireman, said something that stuck with me. "Your Amish background shows."

Somewhat surprised, I asked, "Oh? How's that?"

He said, "Your determination. When I put tests before you, you ace them. You're doing so well because you're here early and never miss a day, and you're invested. I can see the determination on your face."

I thought, 'Wow, I must want it bad enough that others can see I want this.'

Some friends told me, "Eli, you can't drive a truck. Because of where you come from, it will be tough, probably impossible. Amish people don't make good truck drivers." Little did those people know that their doubt motivated me to prove them wrong.

After completing the six-week CDL training program, I scored almost 100 percent on the written CDL exam, which was administered by a retired state highway patrol officer. The test included an extensive checklist of about 120 points for both pre-trip and post-trip inspections on a semi-truck and trailer. Every evening during CDL School, I took the manual home and poured over it for hours. Nikki helped by quizzing me until I had memorized each of the 120-plus steps. I mastered the details of what to inspect and how to identify and describe issues—whether something was cracked, leaking, bent, or worn. I committed to memory every aspect of the pre-trip inspection process required of a truck driver.

On test day, the examiner recognized that I had memorized the inspection list. He said, "You recounted every single point of inspection word for word, just as it is written in the book." He went on, "I know that you really studied that and memorized it." But then he started talking about something entirely different to distract me. When he returned to his questions about the truck, I picked up right where we left off. He shook his head in amazement.

When we finished, he looked at me appraisingly and remarked with a chuckle, "You're one of a kind." Curiosity got the better of him, prompting him to ask, "Where did you come from?"

I told him, "I grew up Amish."

His response was part acknowledgment and astonishment. "Well, that explains your determination. I've never encountered anyone quite like you. Are you even human?"

With a slight smile, I assured him, "I think I am."

The more I read something, the clearer I can see the words in my mind, almost like pictures. This left an impression on my instructor, who was amazed at my ability to memorize and recall information so vividly.

However, the road test presented some challenges for me. Transitioning from inspecting the truck to actually driving it, with the examiner by my side, was quite different from the verbal examination. I fumbled with the gears a bit and coasted out of gear for slightly more than the allowable distance of a full truck length—I believe it was about a truck length and a half. Consequently, my road test portion didn't score as well as I had hoped.

Despite these mistakes, my strong performance in other areas made it difficult for them to justify failing me. The strengths in one aspect of the test compensated for the shortcomings in another, and I passed. I think they understood that my mistakes were due to a lack of experience rather than knowledge. In 2010, I began a new career path as a truck driver.

Recruiters from trucking companies visited the truck driving school to find new graduates like me. Before I knew it, I received multiple job offers. It was an entirely new experience for me that felt a bit intoxicating.

I accepted an offer from Garner Trucking to become an over-the-road (OTR) driver. I spent days on the road, sometimes even longer. My truck became a second home. Two types of trucks travel the highways. Trucks like the one I started with have large cabs that include living quarters for the driver. Then there are day cabs, which have no such amenities and are typically used for local deliveries that allow drivers to return home each night. My initial venture into truck driving involved those long, extended trips, quite different from the local driving I do now.

Getting the job with Garner Trucking was a moment of immense pride for me. My upbringing in the Amish community had never afforded me a sense of achievement quite like this. The skepticism about my ability to pass the CDL exam intensified my sense of accomplishment—I had proven the naysayers wrong! For the first time in my life, I felt like I was worth something. It was as if my existence had been validated.

As significant as this achievement was for me, the praise and admiration I received from Nikki and her family surpassed it. Growing up Amish, I had often battled feelings of inadequacy. Nikki and her family's support and recognition were nothing short of amazing—I finally felt truly accomplished and valued. It was an unforgettable feeling.

44

BANKRUPTCY

For nineteen years after leaving the Amish, I ran from my past, myself, and from Jesus. I wanted no part of anyone who talked about Jesus, God, the Bible, or church. I went on a path of self-deception to find peace from the raging storm within my head. My path led me to make a lot of foolish choices, that included stupid job decisions, substance abuse, and a long list of failed relationships. My pattern of poor decisions eventually led to irreparable financial devastation. When a person is living with emotional pain and turmoil, they'll do anything for relief—even temporary relief— no matter the long-term consequences; I was no exception.

By 2011, I had been an over-the-road truck driver for over a year. With my newfound financial success as a truck driver, I was far too eager to move my family out of my in-laws' house. As an OTR driver, my wife and son were at home alone for days on end. Nikki and I decided to purchase a home. We could not afford the home at the time, but I thought a house would dull my guilt and feed my ego, knowing full well I could not afford a new home. We applied for a loan and got approved, but within eighteen months, we lost the house to foreclosure.

My financial decisions surrounded my self-gratification. I was drinking heavily, going to clubs, strip clubs, and parties—a lot of my decisions financially drained us, just like my father had done to my family growing up. To put it simply, my decisions and pattern of self-indulgence were leading me and my family toward financial ruin.

Things looked hopeless after the bankruptcy. My desperation sent me in a direction I had previously opposed—I decided to pick up the Bible and read it. I'd never read any other Bible besides the Amish German Martin Luther 1522 Bible. So, I picked up the old German Bible that I'd taken with me when I left the Amish and read a couple of verses here and there. Just here and there.

To indulge my flesh, I became heavily addicted to pornography. My wife sometimes caught me because I did it so much. She saw the history of what I was searching for online. My internet habits even caused some viruses on my phone. I was slowly destroying my family, my marriage, and my mind.

By 2015, two years after my bankruptcy, I had read just enough verses in the Bible where I knew of salvation, but I didn't seek God and ask him to reveal it to me. I just immediately started thinking, I've made a lot of bad choices. I have a bankruptcy and I've lost everything, maybe I should just go back to being Amish to make things right with God. But I didn't share this thought with my wife right away. I just knew I needed to make a change.

I felt hollow and empty inside. I had believed I would achieve true freedom and fulfillment by abandoning my Amish roots for the English way of life. But bankruptcy was a financially and emotionally devastating blow—it crushed me. In hindsight, I recognize it was a crucial moment God used to gain my attention. I had chased after what I believed would bring me happiness and success, only to find myself in utter misery and failure. Perhaps it was time to give God a chance.

Spending my nights away from my wife and son, alone in the truck, I tentatively began to explore the Bible. I focused on familiar passages from my Amish upbringing, verses selectively highlighted by the Old-Order Amish to support their doctrines. While searching the Scriptures for answers, I continued to struggle with pornography and alcohol. I sat in my truck, reading my Bible, drinking beer and watching porn. I was acutely aware of the void within me, a missing piece to my life's puzzle, but I remained uncertain of what it was or where to find it.

45

RETURN TO EGYPT

The Book of Exodus tells how God miraculously removed the Israelites from their captivity in Egypt. The Egyptians used them as slaves for over 400 years, working them to death to ensure they wouldn't grow in strength or number. God delivered them by parting the Red Sea, allowing them to escape on dry ground, and then drowning their enemies while they were in hot pursuit. God had prepared a fantastic place for them, but their stubbornness and defiance of God delayed their arrival in the Promised Land. They engaged in self-indulgent, blasphemous behavior in defiance of God after He dramatically rescued them. They complained bitterly to their leader Moses, and completely lost sight of where they had come from—they actually wanted to return to slavery. They felt their lives as slaves were more desirable than having to face the responsibilities that came with the freedom God gave them.

I encourage you to read the Book of Exodus. The Bible contains all the behaviors of humans. If you read enough of it, you'll find yourself within its pages. I sure did.

To ease my guilt and shame, I had begun to read some Scripture from time to time. Growing up, I was taught that you must always follow the Ten Commandments and you must always honor your father and your mother. Those commandments weighed me down. Of course, I couldn't find any verses about the ordinance the Amish church followed. But I was taught that you must be aligned with the Amish church ordinance and rules to please God. Like the Israelites living in the wilderness, I began thinking I needed to return to Egypt. In 2016, I asked my wife and son, "Would you guys be willing to return to the Amish with me?"

To my surprise, my wife responded with unwavering support, "Yes, whatever you want, honey. Let's do it." My son was only about ten years old at the time, but he seemed surprised by the conversation. He remained quiet over the shift in our family's direction.

After my father's suicide, visits to my mother became infrequent. Over the years, my siblings took over the operation of the farm while she continued to live in her home, as she still does today. Eventually, my younger brother, Lester, moved onto the farm with his family. They have taken up the mantle of running the farm and are committed to caring for my mother for the remainder of her life.

During our visits to my mother, we discussed the possibility of my family returning to the Amish community. Seeing her hopes raised at the prospect was heartening. Her smiles returned, and she even began planning to make Amish clothing for my wife, son, and me. I shared with her about my reaching a personal crossroads and my desire to recapture God's approval by returning to the Amish church. Despite my supposed freedom, a sense of peace eluded me, leaving an emptiness that seemed insurmountable. In my desperation, I longed to return to the familiar—to go back to Egypt.

I tried my best, but I still lacked a complete understanding of spiritual salvation. I genuinely wanted to please God. I thought if I returned to being Amish and embraced the ordinance of the church, it would honor my father and mother. God might recognize my effort as a good thing, and I could maybe earn a spot in Heaven. That was my mindset. It was the only hope I saw for salvation at that time.

My mom strongly agreed with my decision to return to the Amish. She affirmed, "Yes, that's your only hope," and she encouraged me with those words. Having her approval was very uplifting. She cautioned me against talking about "salvation," a topic she associated with the outside world, saying, "That's what the worldly people talk about. The prideful world always claims to be saved, and we cannot know that." She emphasized the importance of aligning with the church for forgiveness. "You must be aligned with the church. The church must forgive you of your sins and vote to forgive you. Once you're aligned with the church's ordinance and its rules and keep those rules, they'll vote to forgive you, and then Jesus can forgive you and maybe let you into Heaven," she explained.

She reassured me about my acceptance back into the community: "Eli, when you return, you won't be shunned very long. They'll vote to forgive you because we all love you. You'll be accepted into the Amish church and have a better chance of getting to Heaven."

I asked, "But you're still not sure I'll go to Heaven?"

She answered, "Well, we can never know for sure. Us Amish people can never know for sure that we are going to go to Heaven. We follow the rules and do good works to please God, and then He chooses who He lets in," she said.

I bought into everything she said and started getting ready to go back to Amish. I got rid of everything except for two Ohio State shirts. When it came down to it, I couldn't let them go. I'm a huge college football fan, and my Ohio State Buckeyes mean the world to me. I even have an Ohio State tattoo on my arm.

For our next visit to see my mom, I wore my Amish garb, and so did my wife and son. We were all decked out in Amish clothes, ready to seal the deal on our return to the community. My incredible wife was all in. She had my back, even though she'd have to kick her smoking habit and give up a bunch more besides. She was aware of the tough road ahead but wanted my happiness above all. She was prepared to make those sacrifices. God bless her for that!

We visited my mom to finalize the details of our return. During the visit, I brought up my Ohio State tattoo. The moment she saw it, she burst into tears, "That is an unforgivable sin. Is there any way you can remove that?"

I suggested, "Well, there's laser tattoo removal. I could try."

She questioned further, "But you'll see the imprint even if the ink is removed, right?"

"Yeah," I answered, feeling downcast.

My mom told me how the Amish church made a young man remove a brand mark from a branding iron (used to burn an identifying mark into a cow's hide). He was in a youth group at the time, and in a moment of youthful indiscretion—or maybe it was just plain stupidity—he branded himself with a number. He did it on his upper arm because he thought having an image like that would be cool. He was so prideful that he showed it to everybody, "Just like an animal, I can take it," he bragged.

Continuing her explanation, she elaborated on the Amish view regarding Social Security numbers, which they believe are part of the "beast system." She reminded me that the Ten Commandments include, "Thou shalt not have any other idols or graven image." The Amish consider tattoos as graven images along with photos and videos. My mom's reaction to my tattoo stemmed from her knowledge of the severe community response to the young man who branded himself. He was shunned and excommunicated until he managed to remove the image and the remaining scar.

The young man's method for removing his brand was quite drastic. He resorted to filleting his skin to remove the scar. While it eliminated the branded number and image, it left behind a different kind of scar—a severe, unsightly mark—a large blob. Despite the appearance of this new scar, the Amish community deemed the removal of the original brand sufficient since the image of the number was gone. They considered his actions as adequate repentance. He was forgiven and welcomed back into the church.

My mom made it clear to me that simply removing the ink wouldn't be enough. The remaining image, anything that even remotely resembled the Ohio State logo, would need to be entirely cut away, much like the young man had to remove his brand.

I said, "Mom, I'm very discouraged by this. I have made plans to come back to the Amish. I thought I could please God. Now you've just destroyed that notion." I continued, "Right now, with how you're talking, how the Amish church treats tattooed people, I would have to chop my arm off to come back Amish. I don't think that's love. I don't think you guys want me back."

And with that, Egypt quickly lost its appeal.

46

TURNING POINT

Following the heart-wrenching conversation with my mother, I was consumed by anger, frustration, and a deep sense of bitterness. I stormed off and didn't visit my mother for several years.

I fell back into my old pattern of gratifying my flesh in every way possible. My drinking escalated to the point where Nikki made secretive plans to divorce me. The Bible became a distant memory —I was utterly lost. I didn't know how to please God; I had no idea what He wanted from me.

Then came the day Nikki laid it all on the line: "You have to choose; it's either me or the alcohol. I can't do this anymore." Despite her ultimatum, I couldn't let go of the bottle. Alcohol was my escape. It was my way of dodging reality, but it was costing me everything precious—my wife and my son were slipping away.

In 2017, a year after my failed attempt to return to Amish, I got out of bed late one night and went into the garage of the house we had recently purchased. I started splattering every beer I had; I smashed those cans all over the floor. Beer was everywhere, including on me. It was an act of violence, but this time, it was directed toward the source of my troubles. It dawned on me, 'I'm following my dad's path. I'm wrecking my body with alcohol and tearing apart the lives of those I love.'

Nikki heard the commotion and came out to see what I was doing. She thought I was going off the rails as usual when I got mad in the middle of the night. She figured I was getting drunk again. Confused by what she saw, she asked, "Why are you splattering your beers all over the walls and floor?"

"I don't know exactly," I confessed, "but want to be done with this stuff. I hate it. But I don't know how to stop it."

Tears immediately began to stream down her face. "You're done? You're going to lay it all down? You're going to quit drinking?" she pressed for confirmation.

"Yeah, I want to. I just don't know how. But I will find a way," I affirmed.

Overwhelmed, she shared, "Oh my goodness. I've been praying all night long. I stayed up all night praying and seeking God. I don't want to divorce you, but I have to if you don't stop. Your heavy drinking, your verbal and mental abuse, yelling, screaming at me, belittling me, manipulating me; I can't bear it anymore. I feel like I'm the reason you're drinking, and I feel guilty."

"I've had enough," I said to her. I had been drinking earlier that evening and went to bed drunk. Somehow, I managed to get out of bed with a hangover and started destroying my beers.

'I've been up all night praying for you.'

Hearing Nikki say she'd been praying all night for me was inde-scribable. It felt like I was truly hearing her for the first time, like I was waking up from a dream into actual reality. I had no idea Nikki prayed at all. She was from a nominally Christian background, so this was news to me. But right then, it hit me—there's a God out there who cares about me. The problem was that I didn't know how to believe in Him or even what exactly I should believe about Him. I was clueless about salvation, about what it meant to be saved. Yet, at that moment, I was certain that it was God's power, through my wife's intense prayers, that got me to wake up and destroy my beers. I knew that God did that through my wife. It gave me hope for something beyond my present state and understanding. I didn't know what to do, but I knew there was a path forward, and I had to find it.

47

DISCOVERING TRUTH

After witnessing the power of my wife's prayer, I was convinced God was real and that He responded to my wife's outcry. Realizing that God not only existed but also listened and responded sparked a change in me. Nikki's faith had inspired me, so I reached out to God and pleaded, "God, if you can be with her, bless her, and answer her prayers, then I need Your help too. I need You to respond to me as You did to my wife. I'll read my Bible more and turn away from my sins." So, I did. I started reading the Bible.

True repentance still eluded me. My hunger for pornography remained, my language was still foul, and dishonesty and deceit were part of my daily interactions. I often borrowed money without any intention of repayment. According to the verses I was reading, all these behaviors were sinful. Even engaging in gossip was considered a sin. The Bible's teachings brought me face to face with a deep sense of guilt over these sins, yet I felt powerless to overcome them. I hadn't yet found my identity in Christ. I was power-less against the temptation of my sinful desires.

In my semi-truck, I continued obediently reading the Bible. I just kept reading, and reading, and reading.

One day, I was talking to my cousin, David Yoder, a former Amish, and I shared my frustrations with him. I explained, "I wanted to go back to Amish, but they made me very angry about my tattoo. My mom doesn't accept tattoos. They'd make me cut my arm off just so they couldn't see the tattoo. I want to please God. I've tried to lay down my alcoholism. I've tried to stop sinning. I'm going to go to a different Amish community; I'm not sure where yet. I need to find a way to please God."

David looked at me wisely and said, "Eli, I want you to make me a promise."

"What?" I asked.

"I need you to read an English-written Bible that you can under-stand. I need you to go through the entire thing in depth, every chapter, every verse, every book in the Old and New Testament, and when you finish, do it again."

I looked at him skeptically, "You expect me to do that?"

"Yeah. Promise me you'll do it before joining any Amish community."

I made that promise, "Okay, I'll do it," and I did.

I went to the Goodwill store and bought an NIV translation, English Bible. I started reading the Bible that week. Reading the Bible for the first time in English was freeing. I'd grown up speaking Pennsylvania Dutch and reading the Bible in formal German, which was difficult to understand. By this time, English was my most used language, so it was quite an experience to read the Bible for the first time in a language I could really understand.

When I first started reading the Bible, it didn't make much sense to me. I had run from God for nineteen years after leaving the Amish. Throughout those years, I held to the Amish thinking that it wasn't an individual's responsibility to understand what the Bible says because it wasn't possible. In other words, we were taught that the Bible was intentionally vague and written in a manner beyond the understanding of man. That meant anyone claiming knowledge or understanding of the Bible was obviously deceived by the Devil. That was the logic behind my mindset.

But the day came when the veil of my deception was lifted, and I became undeceived. I went through every verse in the Book of Matthew. I got to where I was speed reading. I got into the Book of Mark and did the same thing. I got into the Book of Luke and did the same thing there. But something hit home in Matthew 10:37-38 (NIV), where Jesus spoke and told His disciples, *"Anyone who loves their father or mother more than me is not worthy of me; anyone who loves their son or daughter more than me is not worthy of me. Whoever does not take up their cross and follow me is not worthy of me."* It made me stop. It made me back up, and I reread it because I was taught you must honor your father and your mother. You must keep the forefathers' tradition of the Amish and honor them in this way to meet the fifth of the Ten Commandments that says to honor your father and your mother.

Then I read Ephesians 6:1, 4 (ESV), which says, *"Children, obey your parents in the Lord. Fathers, do not provoke your children to anger.*" That started connecting in my mind. I thought, '*In the Lord.*' I'm still not finding Amish in here anywhere; I'm still not seeing anything about forefathers and needing to honor them only. But it says, *"Honor them and obey them in the Lord."* I thought, 'Wait a minute, if they're in *religion,* in that *tradition,* they're not in the Lord. So why am I following that? Why am I feeling guilty, and wanting to go back to my Egypt if they're not in the Lord? They're in *ordinance* and *rules.* They worship an organized religion made up by a man.' It started clicking. It was like peeling an onion; one layer after another started coming off.

I read Matthew, Mark, Luke, and then John. In the Book of John, something happened. I didn't recognize it then, but looking back, I can see that I had developed a hunger for truth. I remember sitting in my truck for hours just reading the Bible; I couldn't get enough. It was like discovering food I never knew existed that satisfied a hunger I'd never satisfied. The Book of John was all about Jesus. It was amazing. I got into John and came to chapter 8, verse 32 (ESV), *"If you know the truth, the truth shall set you free."* I looked at that and asked myself, 'What is the truth?' The Devil kept reminding me of Egypt—returning to the Amish—but I was reading about the truth. Well, what's the truth? Is Amish the truth, or is this Bible the truth? I'm not finding anything about being Amish in the Bible, nothing about forefathers. So are the Amish ways the truth, or is this Bible the truth? I started asking God those questions.

I started praying over the Scriptures and asking God to reveal the truth. I was discovering the truth. I wanted to know the truth. I was hungry for the truth. I read how Jesus offered living water to the Samaritan woman at the well. I thought, 'That's me. I'm hungry. I want to know. I'm thirsty, and I want to be satisfied. Why don't you let me know, Lord? Why don't you reveal it all to me, Lord?'

In John chapter 4, Jesus talks with the Samaritan woman. In verse 10 (NIV), Jesus said to the Samaritan woman, *"If you knew the gift of God and who it is that asks you for a drink, you would have asked him and he would have given you living water."* Jesus compared the quenching of physical thirst to the forgiveness of sins. Unlike physical thirst, which needs to be satisfied again and again, Jesus was telling the woman that forgiveness was like living water that satisfied so fully that the person never thirsts again. I began to see my attempts to earn my salvation, like my going into debt, so I could look or feel better about myself. The debt I incurred, like my religious works, had no lasting value and simply added to the accumulation of debt that needed to be paid in the future. The eternal reality of salvation and what it meant started unfolding before me. It was like discovering a hidden treasure!

I came to John 14:6 (NIV), where Jesus said, *"I am the way and the truth and the life. No one comes to the Father except through me."* I remember reading this, and it was like a loose connection got plugged into the right spot. An incredible sense of peace came over me from head to toe. It burned through me with an intense heat. I didn't understand what was happening, but whatever it was, I knew it was real, maybe the most real thing I'd ever encountered. When I read John 14:6, I experienced the baptism of the Holy Spirit and fire, and I received a new heart. It was as if my inner being was being transformed. The old me passed away, and the new me had finally been born. I discovered the truth, and it set me free, just like the Bible said. I became undeceived!

I was so fired up that I kept on reading. I couldn't stop. I went through the rest of the Book of John. I read through Acts; I continued and read through Romans. In Romans 3:23 (NIV), *"for all have sinned and fall short of the glory of God."* Romans 10:9 (NIV), *"If you declare with your mouth Jesus is Lord, and believe in your heart that God raised him from the dead, you shall be saved."* All I could think about was how, 'Nothing says that you must follow your forefathers. Nothing says you must be Amish, or part of a religion, or church, or follow a complicated ordinance.'

I read a King James version of the Bible that day. I'd been reading from seven different versions of the Bible. Many people make an idol out of their favorite translation of the Bible. Religious voices were telling me all sorts of information about different versions of the Bible, telling me I needed to read this version or that version or some other version. But I had all of them. I didn't care what anybody said at that point. I wanted the truth, so I got all of them and read them all.

God directed me to the Book of Colossians in the King James Bible. I was reading Colossians 2, and the entire chapter blew the lid off the Amish religious teaching that had colored my life. The whole thing is about exposing traditions and manmade religion. But by verse 14, I finally saw the word *ordinance* in the King James Bible for the very first time. I thought I had to follow the ordinance, so I read these words very carefully, *"Blotting out the handwriting of ordinances, which was contrary to us, and took it out of the way, nailing it to the cross."* I thought, 'What? Did You tell me that, Lord? Is this really in Your book, in the Bible? Because it says my ordinance that I wanted to go back and follow—back to Egypt— was nailed to the cross.' God's Word had sealed the deal in my mind; it was like I could see for the first time.

That day, I was parked at a truck stop, along with a few hundred other rigs—drivers were resting, eating, or sleeping. I was so over-joyed with this revelation of truth that I jumped out of my truck and went from truck to truck. I went down the row, talking to every truck driver I could find in that entire facility. I asked them if they knew where they were going if they died today. Some of them looked at me stupidly. I told drivers, "I'm dead serious. It's all about Jesus." I said, "It's not about church buildings; it's not about religion or being religious." I said, "I'm not finding religion in the Bible. It's all about Jesus. All my self-righteousness was nailed to the cross. I will no longer do good works to hope I go to Heaven." I told the one guy, "You know what? A dog barks because he's a dog. He doesn't bark to become a dog." I looked in his face and said, "Eli Yoder, he's no longer going to do good works to try to be saved because I am saved." A Christian does good deeds and good works for others, shares the Gospel, and loves others *because* he's saved. He doesn't do good works to *become* saved. I would no longer go back to Egypt. I had lost all desire to return to the bondage and slavery of a religious system. Following the rules and ordinance of the Amish church in hopes I might go to Heaven no longer appealed to me because I had discovered the truth. I was saved right there and then, and I knew it!

That day, the truth was finally revealed to Eli Yoder, and I've never been the same since. I inherited a name in Heaven and on Earth that day. Shortly afterward, people started calling me "The Preaching Truck Driver" because I couldn't keep my mouth shut anymore.

In my enthusiasm over my newfound salvation, I was woefully ignorant of something very important. Salvation was not the destination; it was, in fact, just the beginning of a journey that would test me in ways I could never have imagined.

PART 4

THE PRESENCE OF GOD

48

THE JOURNEY BEGINS

I understood salvation for the first time in my life when I believed through faith, *"For by grace are ye saved through faith; and that not of yourselves: it is the gift of God: Not of works, lest any man should boast"* (Ephesians 2:8-9). I knew that salvation had nothing to do with what I did to please God; it was about what He had already done for me. I understood this promise, and I believed it. I knew that it was by grace alone, by faith alone, and by Christ alone. I knew that I was saved through God's grace and my belief. I understood that I was saved. But I thought salvation was the end of the journey when it was just the beginning.

If I had died at that moment, I knew I would spend eternity with my Lord and Savior Jesus. But just because I understood that salvation came through Jesus Christ didn't mean my bad habits just disappeared like smoke.

You've probably heard people talk about how they came to Christ and all their desires for sin disappeared. Well, praise God for their immediate deliverance! But that's not how things happened to me.

When I first got saved, many things changed in my life. But some of my old habits persisted for several years and set up quite a battle in my mind and spirit. I drank significantly less, but I drank in secret sometimes because I loved alcohol too much to give it up. I continued with occasional pornography and other sinful behavior. I sinned far less than before, but I still did things I shouldn't have. The chains of my sin still held me in bondage, and my secrecy strengthened them. When temptation called to me, I often obeyed.

From the moment of my salvation, I was very vocal about coming to Christ. I wanted to meet the external expectations of what I thought a Christian should look like. The Bible says, *"The fear of the Lord is the beginning of wisdom"* (Proverbs 9:10). But I didn't truly fear what God saw in my heart. At first, I was more worried about what people thought of the things I did—a leftover from my Amish religious heritage. I tried to fight these battles on my own, out of public view. I was held hostage by my pride, I wanted to conceal my weaknesses and fix them with my own strength. I didn't yet understand the power available through Christ.

While I grasped the promises of salvation, I had much to learn.

49

LAUNCHING YOUTUBE

I've touched on this several times throughout my story, and I apologize if it seems I am repeating myself. Still, words aren't adequate to describe the incredible thrill I felt in understanding the freedom Jesus brought to my life. I wish I could plant in your head exactly what I felt growing up without the hope of Heaven and the very real promise of Hell. Transitioning from that perspective to what I knew of Jesus at this point in my life was like waking up from a long nightmare. Have you ever woken up from a bad dream and felt the relief of discovering it wasn't true? Multiply that by 1000, and that's how I felt after becoming *undeceived*. I still carry that same ecstatic joy today, maybe even more, because my relationship with Jesus has grown so much.

It's not weird to share your faith with other people. In my case, it would have been weird not to. Who discovers something so wonderful and then keeps it to himself? *That* would be weird, and it would also be cruel not to share something so powerful and transformative. I could never watch someone dying from thirst while I possessed an unlimited water supply. In the same way, I can't not share my story. Jesus brought life to me, and He'll do the same for anyone who receives Him; that's powerful! But many people suffer because they don't know this simple truth.

Following my salvation and undeception, I sought every opportunity to share my story and tell others about Jesus. I shared with anyone who would listen, even those who would not. On one occasion, I shared my undeception story with a group of Christian truckers. One of the men later encouraged me to share my story on YouTube. I'd been a consumer of YouTube content, but I never imagined myself becoming a YouTube content producer or what later became known as a YouTuber.

I downloaded the apps, and Nikki helped me with some of the technical issues. I recorded my first video—a cringe-worthy production that didn't gain much attention. It was a humble start, for sure. I kept at it since I'm not easily discouraged, or maybe I'm just too stubborn to quit. I made more and more videos and uploaded them to my channel. It was a learning process that took a long time before the channel gained any traction. I think most people would have given up. Growth came slowly in the early years, but a few years later, it exploded.

Eventually, I expanded to Facebook and then to TikTok. My social media outreach grew to something I could never have imagined, allowing me to minister to thousands. It's how I became known as "The Preaching Truckdriver."

50

THE HOUSEHOLD

The choices I made as a husband and father had a direct impact on my wife and son. For many years, my sinful lifestyle heaped oppression, sadness, and financial hardship on my family.

I already told you that I continued to struggle with some of the strongholds in my life. Still, there was an immediate impact that significantly reduced my use of alcohol and pornography, and it had a dramatic effect on my family.

My pornography use had a substantial consequence on my wife, but my alcoholism affected my entire family because my son had to deal with my behavior change every time I got drunk, and sometimes I wasn't very pleasant to be around. It's not possible to have a meaningful relationship with an alcoholic. But when I professed my new faith in Christ, it changed my family. They started going to church with me. I was an over-the-road truck driver at the time, so I couldn't go every Sunday. But when I was home, my wife and my son went with me.

I remember how blessed I was when I saw my son write down scriptures he heard me discuss. He also memorized the Lord's Prayer and other verses from the Bible. The changes in my life also changed him. As often happened in the Bible, when somebody got saved, their whole household got saved. It was a beautiful thing to watch.

My wife claims that the day I got saved was the happiest day of her life and that I became a new person. The old had passed away, and the new in Christ was here. It really made her happy. It also blessed her, my son, and my in-laws. They told me how proud they were of the changes in my life.

Biblically, the husband is supposed to be in charge spiritually, emotionally, and physically. I had not been doing any of those things. I was a drunk and had never really stepped up to the plate and taken charge. I didn't know how to meet my wife's needs— being there for her emotionally, physically, and spiritually as a spiritual leader, according to the Bible. Once the proper order fell into place and I assumed my ordained role, God blessed my marriage; it blossomed like never before. Jesus set my marriage ablaze. I prospered in multiple ways and in many areas of life. Everything was much better, but I still had some lingering issues that dogged me.

51

BAPTISM

Nikki and I both agreed that it was biblical to get water baptized because Jesus was baptized, and we had both come to the saving knowledge of Jesus Christ. My wife wanted to get baptized and said, "I want to do it with you." My son wanted to wait a little. We didn't pressure him to decide. He's still waiting, and I'm hoping and praying that I will baptize my son one day.

We approached our pastor and asked him if he would baptize us. Before he agreed, he sat down with us and ensured we understood the plan of salvation clearly. Then, he explained how baptism represented salvation: you go down into the water, leaving the old and coming up out of the water as a new creation in Christ.

I initially viewed baptism as something I *should* do— 'it'll fix all my lingering problems,' I thought. My pastor talked to me about that. He wasn't forceful or condemning, but I could tell he sensed that I wanted to do it because I still had shortcomings—I still sinned here and there. But he agreed to baptize us.

I thought baptism was a means of gaining an advantage over bondage. I soon realized my thinking was flawed because that would've been considered good works. Ephesians 2:8–9 says: *"For by grace are ye saved through faith; and that not of yourselves: it is the gift of God: Not of works, lest any man should boast."* The Holy Spirit gave me discernment to understand that it would be good works if I were only getting baptized because I should or because it would finally deliver me from all my stuff. I had to focus on Jesus. I got baptized for what Jesus did, not because I must do it as an act of repentance—good works. I had some wrong thinking there. I'm so blessed that Nikki and I were able to get baptized together and draw that line in the sand. That was a momentous milestone.

The impact it had on Nikki was significant. I saw her become much happier after that. Taking that step in faith to get baptized and attend church together made her smile a lot more. She truly began to light up. Her face actually looked brighter. There was a fire in her, and she seemed happier than ever. All these things brought us closer than we'd ever been. It was like our marriage was reborn.

52

PURSUING GOD

Before I received Christ as my Savior, I read the Bible as a religious act to please God. My motive wasn't to seek understanding, and it certainly wasn't to develop a relationship with Him. For many years, Bible reading was a self-righteous, good-works thing I did to make God happy and increase my odds of getting into Heaven, even though I knew my odds weren't very good.

Then I read what Jesus said when He ascended, *"But the Comforter, which is the Holy Ghost, whom the Father will send in my name, he shall teach you all things, and bring all things to your remembrance, whatsoever I have said unto you"* (John 14:26). Reading that made me think, 'If I have that, then certainly I can understand Him because my understanding comes through reading the Bible.'

I stopped considering Bible reading a token religious act to make God smile. I felt something different—God spoke to me through His Word. It felt good, powerful, honest, and satisfying—so I *wanted* to keep reading. It was no longer a forced act but a longing and hunger. It was like the satisfaction I had always felt after being hungry and enjoying a great meal. It quenched my thirst in a deeply satisfying way.

So, I asked, "Lord, what's wrong here? I'm saved, and I understand Your promises. I told You that I believed. I prayed the salvation prayer, Lord, but I'm still doing this and this. All these things are sins—I know that. I don't feel at peace. I don't have a clear conscience. Sin still has a hold on my life, and I can't shake it."

I eventually reached a point of total brokenness. I cried out to the Lord one night from the end of my bed. I said, "Lord, I've already been telling others about what You've done for me. I'm fired up over everything You've done. I know what salvation is now, and You finished it on the cross. I understand all these promises. I'm sharing the Gospel with other people, but I'm still struggling inside. Lord, what's going on here?"

I started crying—bawling, really. After about 20 minutes, I began to get angry. My crying turned into screaming at God. I was angry at God. I yelled at God. I said, "If You are truly who You say You are, why do You not hear me? I'm praying to You. I need to hear from You now! Why do I *feel* unsaved? I believe in salvation. I believe the promises in Your Word. I know Jesus finished it. But why do I still *feel* like I'm not saved? I don't have a clear conscience. I still *feel* dirty. What's wrong?"

Finally, in frustration, I cried out, "I'm not hearing from You, Lord. I'm going to go to bed now." I threw my Bible on the floor in defeat, and I told God, "I'm never going to read that Bible again until I hear from You." I was exhausted and fell asleep.

The following day, my alarm went off. I had just opened my eyes. I hadn't even brushed my teeth yet or gotten dressed. I just opened my eyes, and out of my mouth came a Bible verse. At least, I was reasonably sure it was a Bible verse. Some people might find this hard to believe, but God spoke to me by putting a Bible verse into my mind while I was sleeping. It was as if it were programmed and downloaded into my brain while sleeping. The best way I can explain it to you is that I could see it. Not only could I speak it, but I could see it. It was in all capital letters. I could almost taste it. I could think it. I could say it. But I knew I had never memorized it before.

I woke up crying again, but this time, I was crying tears of joy because I knew that I had received something from Almighty God. How did I know that verse?

I grabbed my phone and searched Google for the verse word for word. What I had spoken from my lips was Matthew 6:33 (ESV): *"Seek first the Kingdom of God and his righteousness, and all these things shall be added to you."*

Something powerful happened to me that day. I realized there was more to be had. I didn't know what it was, but I was prepared to keep looking, seeking, and continuing to pursue God's truth.

53

SURRENDER

I was invited to the Church of God in West Liberty, Ohio by Tracy and Eric. They were friends we had met at the New Hampshire Community Church. I didn't want to go at first. I put it off a couple of times, but discernment kept coming back. The Lord wouldn't let me forget it. "Hey, your friends invited you. Why do you keep finding excuses not to go?" I didn't quite understand the spiritual battle I was facing or about taking thoughts captive. But I knew that God wanted me there and that if I didn't obey, I would be resisting God. I couldn't get it out of my mind. That's what finally caused me to obey God.

The experience helped me begin to develop discernment. I started to recognize when the Lord put something weighty in my heart, especially when it caused me to wake up from a deep sleep in the middle of the night. When the revelation hit me, I repented. "Oh, Lord, I'm so sorry. I'm so sorry for disobeying You. I will go. I don't know which Sunday yet, but okay, Lord, I'll go." I could no longer avoid obedience to this calling. There's no question what you need to do when you receive Holy Spirit discernment. That thought is there. 'You must go.' I later recognized all the negative thoughts that said, 'Oh, you're afraid of people. You shouldn't go.' That was from the enemy. It was good versus evil in the spirit realm.

I had never been to an altar at any church because I was always worried about what people would think of me. "Why is he going forward?" I finally went to the church, and I met everybody. I met Tracy and Eric. I don't remember meeting anybody who recognized me, but I kept thinking, 'Oh, I'm on social media. There are probably a lot more people here who know me.'

The church service was longer than I'd ever experienced, but the time seemed to go by quickly. It didn't finish until after 1:00 p.m. I remember feeling like it was only a 20-minute service. I looked up and thought, 'Wow, it is 1:00 p.m. We had started at 10:30 a.m. I can't believe this.' I'd never been part of a spirit-filled church service like that. In my prior experience, church services ran by a tightly scripted agenda that was precisely timed from start to end. But this church was way different. The preacher just kept preaching. There were long-haired hippies in there. There were people with hats and ball caps worn backward. I saw people with tattoos all over their arms. Some people looked like they came off the streets from homeless shelters or fresh from prison. I thought, 'I like this. I fit right in with these people.'

When the service ended, they kept playing "Amazing Grace.". Anyone who wanted prayer went up to the altar. They prayed over people for all sorts of reasons. I saw person after person go forward. I thought, 'I'm not going up there because people will look at me differently.' I was worried about people. And then the Lord prompted me to go forward. "You have to go forward." I felt the need, but I resisted two very strong urgings. In my mind, I could hear people saying, 'What does he need repentance from? Why is he going forward?'

The third time I felt the urge to go forward and resisted, my knees became very, very heavy, like I was in chains. I couldn't feel anything from my knees down—I was numb. Out of nowhere, an older lady stood by me and said, "Sir, you need to go to the altar." She grabbed my arm, pulling me to my feet. I still couldn't feel my legs, but I obediently staggered down the aisle. To this day, I don't know who that lady was. Later, I wanted to find her and speak with her. I looked at the video recording later, and there was no lady. God supernaturally sent her to me. She grabbed my arm and walked me to the altar. When I got there, I got down on my knees.

I was immediately surrounded by pastors and prayer warriors. 'Why? What for, Lord?' I wondered. They laid hands on me. I felt one hand on my head, another on my shoulder, my other shoulder, the middle of my back, and then I lost count. I was covered with hands, and they were praying. I didn't know what they were praying, but I fell on my face, flat on the floor. The Lord took me flat on the ground at Jesus' feet. I never intended to fall. It was as if an unseen force—the hand of God—brought me to the ground. All thoughts of embarrassment had disappeared. I thought, 'Lord, what do you want from me? What am I here for?' He said, "Now you're going to give me everything and live in my presence." I just started bawling. I said, "Okay, Lord. I know You died on the cross for my sins. I know I don't have to be religious, and I don't have to follow rules—I know this. I gave You my sins, but now I give You my everything, and I want to live in Your presence." God wouldn't let me move until I finished surrendering it all.

While these people prayed, I felt an overwhelming peace come upon me, starting in my head and moving down into my feet and toes. I felt cleansed all the way through. Whatever I was struggling with just left right out of my body. The course of my life changed that day as I encountered the presence of God in a significant and powerful way. I knew His promises, but that day, I understood the power of His presence. I realized I had been standing in my own way, but I had surrendered to God's way.

54

MINISTERING FROM WEAKNESSES

After the West Liberty Church experience, I began releasing my secret sins from the closet by sharing them within the church. I divulged my struggles of returning temptations and even telling lies. My secrets held power over me, and as I released and shared them, the grip they once had on me began to loosen. Meanwhile, I preached against the things I was struggling with personally, although most people didn't know my struggles. I wanted people to know that they could be delivered from the bondage of sin even after being saved. I wanted to minister to them despite my weakness because I knew God had spoken to me that day at West Liberty Church. I'd given Him my sins, but He wanted my whole life. He wanted to provide me with power. Through the power of His presence, He wanted to give me authority over those things. He didn't want me to be miserable while waiting for Heaven.

I shared the power of surrender with other Christians. I realized many people felt comfortable just going to church because they thought they were pleasing God. Lots of folks are just Sunday

Christians. They understand the promises of God, but they know nothing of His presence. When I began to share my weaknesses with others, and tell what happened at that church in West Liberty, people had tears flowing down their cheeks as I told my testimony. Through the power of God's presence, I saw people set free from burdens they'd carried for many years as Christians.

I had the opportunity to lay hands on people and pray for the Holy Spirit's fire to burn through their hearts and for the presence of God to come upon their lives. I asked the Lord to do for them what He had done for me while I was flat on my face at that altar. I prayed they would encounter the presence and peace of God. All glory to God—Many people experienced a similar encounter with God's presence. It wasn't what I did but what God did through me.

God used my testimony to peel layers off people I met face-to-face as a truck driver. Before I knew it, they were standing on the loading dock, surrendering their struggles because of my testimony. That's why Revelation 12:11 says, *"they overcame him by the blood of the Lamb and by the power of their testimony."* Testimonies are powerful!

55

THE LAST SECRET

I made it my mission to liberate myself from secrecy and use my weaknesses to minister to others. Only a few months into my journey, I suffered a humiliating and shameful defeat.

My drinking was under control, but I still had a few beers now and then. I went to my son's football game on a Friday night. For reasons I can't explain, I went for the hard stuff that night and drank whiskey. I was still struggling with alcohol addiction, but I thought I could manage it. Most of the time, I was strong. I could say, "Nope, I'm not doing it, Devil." Those little moments of victory made me feel confident. I slipped into old habits that night. I felt shameful. I felt like Adam and Eve must have felt when they experienced shame for the first time and found fig leaves to cover themselves. That's the way I felt—shameful, embarrassed, and eager to hide.

I made a total fool out of myself at the football game that Friday. People from the church noticed I had been drinking and commented. To make things even worse, I embarrassed my son in front of his friends.

I didn't go to church that Sunday because I was too ashamed. I had fallen. I had messed up. I had disappointed my brothers and sisters. A lot of the guilt from my Amish upbringing resurfaced. 'They're going to shun me. They're going to call me out and shame me.' The Devil tried to convince me that I was a fraud, a defect, and an unredeemable failure. That's what the Devil does—he's the accuser of the brethren. But the truth was quite the opposite.

I finally worked up the courage to go back to church and face whatever was going to happen. To my surprise, my brothers in Christ loved me and prayed for me. They didn't even bring up what happened. When I finally mentioned it to them, they told me they knew I was struggling and had been praying for me all along. They were willing to pray for me, which lines up with Proverbs 24:16 (ESV), *"For the righteous falls seven times and rises again, but the wicked stumble in times of calamity."* When I read verses like that, it made me want to fire right back. 'I'm not staying down. I'm not going to do that.'

My choice to go back to church and not retreat with my secret sin turned out to be a pivotal decision. The love I received from my brothers and sisters was biblical, but it still shocked me; it wasn't what I expected. I expected condemnation and rebuke. Instead, I received love. They weren't loving or accepting of my sin, but they loved me as a person created in the image of God. It wasn't just their love; God's love was poured on me in a life-altering moment. It broke something off me. The power of this loving act drove me straight into the arms of Jesus like never before. The last secret was out, and I had been laid bare. I had survived, and I wasn't going back into the closet.

From that day forward, I changed my approach. I no longer relied on my strength to fix my problems, I looked to Jesus to take my struggles from me. I knew He would give me power over them and teach me how to pray. I learned how to attack alcoholism and take dominion over my addiction by cutting it off at the roots in Jesus' name. I learned to use the authority of Jesus' name to cast out anything that came against me.

I started praying this way because Jesus said, "You will do the things that I'm doing, and even greater things shall you do than I." I thought, 'Are you kidding me, Jesus? You have the greatest power in all of Heaven and Earth. You healed lepers and cast out devils. You're telling me I can do greater things than that?'

I began seeking the Kingdom through the Word of God, and the Holy Spirit led me to John 15:4: when we abide in Jesus, and He abides in us, then we can do all things. I understood the significance of this verse in a new and powerful way. I realized that knowing the promises of God wasn't enough; I also needed His presence in my life. The Bible says He will prune us. Matthew 6:33 says to *seek* Him and His righteousness. I knew that if I read the Word daily, all these things would be added to me. So, I sought His presence every single day by reading the Word. I made more time for God than for myself or anybody else. Reading my Bible was no longer a religious task. I knew I didn't need to earn my salvation by reading it. It was out of a desire to abide in His presence. He gave me peace and the power to live above sin.

After spending time in the Word, I became convicted about my words. *"Life and death are in the power of the tongue"* (Proverbs 18:21). When I read that verse, I shifted my focus from how to please God to what Christ already did for me. I studied the biblical examples of what He had done for others. Then, I trusted Him to do the same for me. I realized I could trust Jesus to help me repent and sanctify me through His Spirit. I knew I wasn't strong enough to do it on my own. I needed His strength, presence, and supernatural power.

I was in the Word daily, and I discovered that I had the power to stop gossiping. I had the power to keep lies from flowing from my lips. I had power over alcohol. But the source of this power was from God, it wasn't my own. When I realized that He died on the cross and defeated the Devil once and for all, I began to understand that *I can do all things through Christ Jesus who strengthens me* (Philippians 4:13 NKJV). I understood that if I stayed connected to the source of power, I would always be able to access it when I needed it. I knew I didn't have enough power in my flesh. The Bible says *flesh and blood shall not inherit the Kingdom of God.*

I no longer had to be a slave to that sin. I once obeyed it, and I realized every time I obeyed it, I was a slave to it. I learned to take dominion and make the problem my slave. I made alcohol and pornography obey me. I spoke to the problem. *With life and death being in the power of my tongue,* I began to speak my future into existence before I saw it take shape. I cast all sin out of my life in the name of Jesus.

Once I took dominion over what once had power over me, I was able to help others. I have used the Word of God and my testimony to help many overcome their struggles, both Amish and English.

If He did it for me, He would certainly do it for them, too. It's what God did for me, not about what I did. That's why God allowed my testimony to play out publicly so that I could help others who struggle with pornography, secret sin, and shame. I challenge and encourage people to leave their shame and enter a lifestyle of abiding in the presence of God.

56

IT NEVER ENDS

Being saved is a one-time event when you come to the knowledge of the truth—it's a gift of God. But sanctification —being set apart by God and remade—is a lifelong process. It didn't stop the day after people prayed over me. It's an ongoing process that results from abiding in the presence of God. It will only stop if I stop reading the Word because the Word of God is the food my soul needs. It's alive and active. It is my source of power and strength.

I want you to understand that reading the Word is absolutely necessary. It's not an option or luxury. You must read the Word of God every day and live in God's presence. Before I crawl out of bed in the morning, I first ask Him to lead me. Every word that I speak must be from Him. Anything that is from the Devil must be cut off now, in Jesus' name. This is not a burden; it is quite the opposite: it's a source of liberty and peace. A person can be saved and remain quite miserable apart from the steady nourishment from the Word of God.

Every word I speak and every thought I think must be brought under the obedience of Jesus Christ. There must be a daily submission to the Lord. In addition to seeking God first every day, the very next verse says, *"Therefore do not be anxious about tomorrow, for tomorrow will be anxious for itself. Sufficient for the day is its own trouble"* (Matthew 6:34). Only worry about today. The Lord revealed to me that I must die to myself every day. I must give myself, my all, my words, my sins, all of me to Him by spending time in His presence. And that's what I pray over my son and my wife daily. I plead the blood of Jesus from head to toe over my family so the enemy cannot affect them. Sanctification continues as I abide in the presence of God. The Holy Spirit manifests in my life over time—and becomes more powerful in me. The Holy Spirit gives Godly wisdom, knowledge, and discernment. There is no arrival, no completion—not in this life. Sanctification is a lifelong journey that I must maintain. As I draw nearer to God, He draws nearer to me. It is impossible to be too near to God!

Understanding and receiving the promises of God will save you. Abiding in God's presence through prayer and the Word of God will bring victory and success every single day. God's promises are not a substitute for His presence; His presence brings power. This understanding and realization changed my life as it will for anyone who grabs hold of it.

PART 5

LIVING UNDECEIVED

57

MY MOTHER

Fellowship and intimacy with God are more incredible than any self-indulgent human behavior. It's better than food, drugs, sex, alcohol, and anything else you can think of. I was so thrilled with my newfound understanding that I wanted everyone I loved to have the same understanding.

My first thought was for my mom. 'By hearing my story about how I got saved and the supernatural experience that I had at the West Liberty church, certainly, she would be persuaded,' I thought. I couldn't wait to tell her! I wanted to share the revelation God showed me in Matthew 6:33. I knew from reading Revelation 12:11 that *"they overcame by the blood of the Lamb and by the power of their testimony."* I wanted to share what had happened to me with my mom—I wanted to tell her my testimony.

I showed up at her house brimming with happiness, all pumped up and on fire, thinking my mom was going to be blown away by what happened to me. 'Maybe she'll want to get saved,' I thought. 'Maybe she'll seek God the same way I did.'

I didn't get very far into telling her about my transformation when she said, "No. No, don't talk about that salvation stuff. That's what the worldly people believe."

I said, "But Mom, my English Bible says the same things as your Martin Luther German Bible does."

"Yeah, but we're not supposed to read the Bible," she countered.

"Why not?" I asked. "Salvation is in there. Ephesians 2:8-9 says, *'For by grace are ye saved through faith.'* It's all there."

But she was unwavering in her position, "Yeah, it's there, but the elders of the church and the bishop tell us that we're not allowed to interpret that as salvation. We can't claim that we're saved from anything. Doing so means the Devil is trying to deceive us and pull us away from our church—God's church, the Amish. The Amish people are God's true church, and we must follow whatever the elders, the bishop, and our ordinance say." She continued, "You can't simply lean on salvation. You must have rules and be aligned with the ordinance of the Amish church—that's the only true way."

I finally accepted that my mom was not going to receive what I said, at least not easily. She wanted no part of salvation and had no interest in understanding the Bible.

On another visit, I pressed the boundary by bringing an English Bible with me in which I had highlighted every salvation verse. I asked her to read the same verses in her German Bible. I even went through the verses with her. When I finished, I asked, "Mom, do you understand it?" And she replied, "No, I don't care to. So please don't speak of salvation anymore."

For several years, I followed my mom's rules and put on Amish clothing to visit her about once each year. My son and my wife also came with me for some visits. It wasn't mandatory for them to wear Amish clothing like I did, but she required it of me. She said that every year, she wanted me to visit to catch up on things, see how they're doing on the farm, and tell her how I'm doing in the non-Amish world. My mom was okay with those visits. But that all changed on her birthday, March 7th, 2024.

We hadn't visited for a while, so I asked my wife when she thought we should go. She suggested going on my mother's birthday to show her love and respect and bring her a birthday card. Even though I had been away from the Amish for twenty-six years, I wanted my mother to know that I still remembered her birthday and I remembered every one of my siblings' birthdays. I thought it would be a unique gesture and a blessing for her. I genuinely love and care about my mom, and I love my siblings, too. They're often on my mind.

We showed up at my mom's house with a beautiful card and my wife and I wrote in it. I'm amazed at how God puts things in my spirit. I wrote things on the card, not knowing what I was going to hear that day. I wrote things about how I really love her as a son. "Though we live different lives, I want you to know I love you even though I chose a life that you disapprove of." And then I said, "I think it's very important that we love the way Jesus loves, even though we live in different cultures. But how do we love like Jesus?" Then I shared John 13:34 (NKJV), where Jesus says, *"Now I give you a new commandment that you love one another. Just as I have also loved you, love one another."* I wrote that in the card and told her that I wanted to love her the way Christ loves, even though I disagree with the Amish rules and the Amish religion, "I love you because I cannot claim to be a Christian if I don't love you the way

Jesus loves you—the way Jesus loved the religious people and wanted to minister to them. And the way Jesus loved sinners and met the woman at the well and the adulterous woman whom he didn't condemn." I wrote all that, and pretty quickly, the left side of the birthday card filled up. I really wanted to show the differences between religious rejection and love—the love of Christ. We all signed it: Nikki, Johnathan, and Eli. Below that I wrote: "We love you. Happy birthday."

My wife and I went by ourselves. Johnathan stayed home because he said, "She never talks to me when I go, and she speaks German to Dad. I don't understand what she's saying. It's just frustrating. She never acknowledges me or asks how I'm doing, so I'm going to stay home. I don't feel loved when I'm there."

We parked at the pallet shop because we couldn't drive a worldly car onto her property. As we walked toward the house, I could smell fresh fried pies through the screen door. I was thinking about those maple clusters and all those goodies she usually made when we came to visit. "Oh, we're about to experience some fried pies," I told my wife.

When we were about five feet from the door, we heard Mom scream from the inner room at the top of her lungs, "No, do not come in. Do not come back. You're not welcome here anymore."

I said, "Mom, it's your birthday." I spoke through the screen door. I never saw her with my eyes. I said, "Mom, I just wanted to give you a card on your birthday."

"Nope. Don't bring it in. Why did you even show up?"

I said, "It's your birthday. That's why we showed up."

After some further exchange, I knew we had to leave, so I laid the card on the porch beside the door. I said, "Okay, Mom, I will just put it right here. "Normally, we could visit you one time each year, and I wanted to show up on your birthday to say happy birthday."

"Just go. Just go."

So we left.

My wife got very angry because she felt the pain that I felt from my mother's hurtful words. She was very upset, and I told her, "I knew this day was coming."

She asked, "What do you mean?"

"I'm going to investigate, but I'm near certain that I know what happened. We're going to find out that Mom is cutting us off for the rest of her life because she found out about my videos talking about the Amish tradition, what happened in our home, the abuse, and what happened to her. She found out what I said about her daddy, the bishop, his behavior, the power and control he had, the shunning, and how she came to him about Dad's drinking, so they shunned my dad, her own husband. She knows that such behavior is not okay in the outside world, and she also knows there could be legal implications."

I started talking with taxi drivers for the Amish. I even spoke with my brother who is in the New Order Amish, and determined that what I suspected was true. One of the drivers (he told me not to mention his name) said, "Hey, I was out getting eggs from your mom, and she asked, 'Have you seen Eli's videos?'" He had, but he didn't want to offend her and lose her business, so he said, "No, but I can keep an eye on it and look to see what's out there." But he had already seen my videos. He knew what I was doing. He told me she continued by saying, "A lady showed up to buy some baked goods, and she said, 'Oh, so you're that famous mother that I saw in the video.'"

Mom asked her, "Where are you seeing me on a video?"

"Well, your son is on social media talking about you."

I told my wife that it was inevitable that she would find out because I have a large audience between TikTok, Facebook, and YouTube. Some of those videos have 30 million views across all platforms. Somebody in that 30 million is going to say something to my mom. I just didn't know when, so I wasn't shocked when I heard mom say what she said through the screen door, because people like to talk. Some of her English customers who buy chicken and baked goods and candies from my mom were eventually going to say something to her because I have shared videos about my experience visiting her. The Amish are okay if you take a side picture or a picture of their back. I did do that with my mom, not face-to-face, because that would be disrespectful.

I did take a couple of photos in my former Amish home. There were lots of comments about how clean and how awesome my mom's house was. The floors and walls were spotless. I loved showing people how good my mom's work ethic was and how much time she put into cleaning her house. I would love for my mom to find out about the compliments she received. But she didn't take it as a compliment when people—her customers, English customers— started talking about seeing videos showing her inside her house. They were so amazed by the video I showed that they wanted to start doing business with my mom and buying her baked goods because they saw the cleanliness of her house.

I'm not upset with those who shared the information with my mom because they meant it as a compliment to her. They couldn't anticipate my mom's telling me, "Do not ever, ever step foot back on this property. Do not come to my funeral when I die." She said these things because of what I did by talking about their way of life. That exposure was a deep wound to her, and I knew this could happen because her daddy, the bishop, made it very clear that Amish traditions are preserved through secrecy. They protect each other and the Amish church by keeping the inner workings private and taking care of their own problems. They don't talk about how they forgive, how they handle criminal acts, and repeat offenders who might get many years in prison in the non-Amish world. My mom's Amish community doesn't want those details leaking out. They don't want the risk of outside authorities getting involved and taking away what they've preserved from their Anabaptist ancestors, people who migrated from Switzerland to escape persecution. They look up to those people.

There's a book called Martyrs Mirror. The book names hundreds, if not thousands, of Amish or Anabaptist forefathers—that's where the Amish come from—who died for their beliefs. They keep those traditions today, and they're willing to die for those beliefs. The only way they can maintain their beliefs is through secrecy, and this means not educating the outside world.

Years ago, maintaining secrecy within the Amish community was simpler. The Amish population was smaller, and the few who left rarely had a platform to share their experiences. But times have changed. Today, countless former Amish, myself included, are openly discussing the hidden realities of Amish life, and there's no silencing us. On social media alone, I'm reaching millions across more than fifty countries, exposing the truth about the Amish church and religious deception in general. Men like my granddaddy, Bishop Levi Beachy—my mother's father—were so determined to protect their secrets that they enforced silence through the threat of societal exclusion (shunning and excommunication) and the fear of eternal damnation. These powerful forms of control aren't exclusive to my former Old-Order Amish community. It's a tool of deception used for thousands of years by the Devil himself, wielded by tyrants, secret societies, oppressive governments, and other religious groups to suppress truth while maintaining power and control over people. The end goal is always the same: to keep people away from the simple truth that Jesus will set them free. Though my story comes from my Old-Order Amish background, the underlying tactics are universal.

As a former Amish who is living undeceived, the Amish church has no control over me because shunning is of no consequence. I will speak the truth so that lies are exposed, and people can be set free. But in my mom's heart, this is a great offense, because, in her eyes, it's the worst sin a person could commit. In my mother's heart, she sees my speaking truth as the ultimate betrayal. It was bad enough for me to leave the Amish, but to talk about their traditions, their way of life, their behavior—how they keep everything hush-hush— that was the greater offense. The stories about my dad and the rules that we had—that was not all that offensive. The greatest offense is talking about the church system, shunning, rejection, and suicide— revealing the secrets.

When I talked about my dad's suicide and how the church condemned him and segregated his grave in the cemetery, that exposed the church and how they think. It showed how they pronounce judgment upon individuals on God's behalf, an action that is so dehumanizing that people end their lives by suicide. For my mom to find out that I talked about such things and exposed their cult of lies is deeply offensive. They know that what they do is not acceptable in the larger world in which they live. They don't want to be persecuted, like their forefathers, so they keep these things secretive. But they're ready to die for their beliefs, just the way the Anabaptists did.

When you put your faith in man-made systems such as the ordinances of a church, you cannot know the only way, the truth, and the life. No one comes to the Father except through Jesus (John 14:6). By trusting in rules, religion, and human traditions, you remain willfully ignorant of the truth, and you lose your way.

Anything that comes from our lives that brings glory to God is because of the grace of our Lord Jesus Christ. John 1:16 says, *"And of his fulness have all we received, and grace for grace."* In 1 Corinthians 15:10, Paul says, *"But by the grace of God I am what I am: and his grace which was bestowed upon me was not in vain; but I laboured more abundantly than they all: yet not I, but the grace of God which was with me."*

Sadly, many people are like my mother. They receive the grace of God in vain because they think we do the best we can and hope that the grace of God will take care of the rest. But anything in our lives that isn't of grace is not of faith, *and whatsoever is not of faith is sin.* It's a sin in God's eyes if we don't have faith because Hebrews 11:6 tells us if we don't have faith, it's impossible to please God. If we don't believe that Jesus finished everything on the cross, that is sin. That is why God allows trials in our lives to wean us from self-confidence and to teach us to trust Him.

Philippians 3:3 says, *"For we are the circumcision, which worship God in the spirit, and rejoice in Christ Jesus, and have no confidence in the flesh."* I was born and raised with confidence only in our good works, in our flesh, our rules, our ordinances, and our Amish traditions. When I read about not having confidence in the flesh, it set me free.

"I am crucified with Christ: nevertheless I live," Paul said. *"Yet not I, but Christ lives in me: and the life which I now live in the flesh I live by the faith of the Son of God, who loved me, and gave himself for me. I do not frustrate the grace of God: for if righteousness come by the law, then Christ is dead in vain"* (Galatians 2:20-21).

If you're going to live by the rules and the law and the ordinance, then Christ died in vain—He died for nothing.

"He that speaketh of himself seeketh his own glory: but he that seeketh his glory that sent him, the same is true, and no unrighteousness is in him" (John 7:18).

I continue to hold out hope for my mother's salvation. I pray that the eyes of her understanding will be opened and that her hunger for truth might override her grip on tradition.

58

MY FATHER

It was around 2008, about five years after my father's suicide. My mind remained filled with questions, especially about what had happened that fateful Saturday morning when he ended his life with a gunshot to the head. No one knew about my secret Sunday morning meetings with him or his plans to leave the Amish community on the day he died. I struggled to understand why my father would end his life when freedom was so close.

I had been visiting my mother periodically over the years, donning my Amish clothes and parking my worldly car at the pallet shop to walk the short distance to her house. During this particular visit, I gradually steered the conversation toward the day my father died. I knew he hadn't died immediately and that he was conscious for some time. But I still had no idea what actually happened that morning. Who had found him? What exactly happened when they did? I didn't want to bring up the painful topic, but it had been five years, and Mom seemed willing to talk about it, so I pressed forward.

It was still a very emotional topic for her, as you can imagine. It was a shocking and painful moment for her. I simply asked, "Mom, would you mind telling me who found Dad first and what made you realize he had attempted suicide? Did anyone hear the gunshot?"

Her voice was shaky, but she persisted. "Yes, we did hear the gunshot, but we waited more than an hour before looking to see who might have fired it."

This may sound strange to some, but occasional gunfire wasn't unusual. Sometimes people in the area would shoot for practice, and other times for hunting. It wasn't unusual for one of my brothers to grab the .22 rifle and go squirrel hunting. Guns were also used to dispatch sick animals, to end their suffering with a clean shot from the .22. Because of this, she didn't find the gunshot suspicious at first. But she did tell me that they had heard it while she was inside the house.

She went on to say that my brother, Lester, came into the house and asked her, "Did you hear that gunshot earlier?" That question raised her concern, as she had thought Lester might have taken the .22 and shot something. Together, they went to the closet, and there it was, hanging in its place.

Now they were both concerned. It had been an hour or more since the gunshot. Thinking someone might be hunting on the property, my mother said to Lester, "How about you go see who it was?" That's when Lester walked around the back of the barn and found my father in a terrible state. He immediately turned around, ran back to the house, and tried to tell Mom. Understandably, he was hysterical, stammering as he tried to explain what he had just discovered. Then Mom went with him to see for herself.

Mom said they walked around the corner of the barn and both began crying at the horror before them. Because it had been so long since the gunshot, she described how his head was swollen to three times its normal size and there was blood everywhere. She recounted saying, "Dad, why did you do this? You know you go to hell if you kill yourself." Hearing her condemnation saddened me at the time. But then she told me something that gave me a spark of hope for my dad's soul, though I didn't fully understand why until years later.

She said she heard him praying after telling him, "You're condemned to hell for that. You can't shoot yourself, Dad." To her surprise, she heard him praying the Lord's Prayer in German. He was confessing his sins, confessing everything he had ever done wrong—all the times he got drunk, everything—he was confessing it all to Jesus. Then he confessed the very sin he had just committed: shooting himself in the head with a .38-caliber pistol.

She told me they saw the pistol lying on the ground beside him. Lester got it away from him. They had no idea he even had that gun. He must have purchased it from someone and hidden it.

Mom told Lester to run to the pallet shop and use the English phone to get help. It was a warm day in June, so the back door to the pallet shop was open, and they had already heard Lester and Mom's screaming. The owner of the pallet shop had started walking toward the commotion to see what was wrong. Lester called out, "Hey, can you call 911?"

When the paramedics arrived, Dad was still alive but losing consciousness, probably due to massive blood loss and the growing pressure against his brain. Mom said she disagreed with the Life Flight decision, but the paramedics called in the helicopter and took him straight to St. Rita's Medical Center in Lima, Ohio. That's where this story intersects with what I wrote previously, when Nikki and I were at the car dealership that same morning.

Mom told Lester to call Levi, who by that time had moved to the New Order Amish community in Tennessee. Then Levi called me while I was at the car dealership.

I remember looking at my mom's face and seeing the pain. She didn't see any value in my dad's confession. She clearly didn't believe that God could forgive him for what he had done, even though he was alive long enough to confess his sins—like the thief on the cross beside Jesus, who acknowledged Him and was saved, going to be with Him in paradise that very day.

Mom believed the church had to vote to forgive someone, that forgiveness was in their hands. She clearly believed my dad was in hell for what he had done, because she was programmed to believe that the Amish church is God's church, and they do the judging for Him. When someone is shunned and shows remorse, all baptized church members must vote on whether the person is forgiven. Until every baptized member votes yes, only then are they forgiven. Since that didn't happen with my dad, she remains in agreement with the Amish bishops and their excommunication letter read over him at the cemetery.

But even then, although I did not yet understand salvation, I felt relieved knowing of his confession. Hearing this from my mom gave me some relief from the pain I had held in my heart for the prior five years.

When I got saved in 2017, I began rejoicing and praising God for my dad's confession. I actually praised God for allowing my father to have this opportunity. All bad things can be used for the glory of God. What the enemy used to steal, kill, and destroy, God used for

His glory and His good. That's when the Lord showed me that He can save a soul, even after an attempted suicide. He saved my dad.

I kept my rejoicing to myself in future visits with Mom because I didn't want her to know that I was going to pick him up the next day. I've never told her because it would only cause more pain. No good would come from it.

Many denominations condemn people for suicide, but I can tell you what the Bible says in 1 John 1:9: *"If we confess our sins, He is faithful and just to forgive us our sins and cleanse us from all unrighteousness."* That's exactly what my dad did before he died. He confessed his sins before the Lord. Clearly, my dad was saved in the final minutes before he became unconscious and passed from this world. Now, a lot of religious people have their own requirements, traditions, and teachings, passed down through generations, that condemn people for the act of suicide.

Are those who die instantly—not able to confess their sins like my dad did—condemned to hell? Not necessarily.

It's a sad fact that some Christians have committed suicide. Adding to the tragedy is the false teaching that committing suicide automatically consigns one to hell. Many believe that a Christian who commits suicide wasn't saved in the first place. This teaching is not supported by the Bible. The Bible teaches that from the moment we truly believe in Christ, we are guaranteed eternal life. John 3:16 states, *"For God so loved the world, that He gave His only begotten Son, that whosoever believeth in Him should not perish, but have everlasting life."* Christians can know beyond any doubt that they possess eternal life. Romans 8:38-39 says, *"And I am convinced that nothing can ever separate us from God's love. Neither death nor life, neither angels nor demons, neither our fears for today nor our worries about tomorrow—not even the powers of hell can sepa-*

rate us from God's love. No power in the sky above or in the earth below—indeed, nothing in all creation will ever be able to separate us from the love of God that is revealed in Christ Jesus our Lord." A Christian who commits suicide is a created being. Therefore, not even suicide can separate a Christian from God's love. Jesus died for all our sins. And if a true Christian, in a time of spiritual attack and weakness, commits suicide, their sin is covered by the blood of Christ Jesus.

Religious people like to distinguish one sin from another. But if you commit one, you've committed them all. When you're born again, you're forgiven for all your sins. But religious people love to condemn others for certain sins and weigh one sin against another. They don't see their own sin of adultery when they're cheating on their spouse. They don't acknowledge the little white lies they told in church last Sunday. They don't view their own sins as significant, but they sure love pointing the finger at others!

According to the Bible, suicide is not what determines whether a person gains entrance into heaven. If an unsaved person commits suicide, they have done nothing but expedite their journey to hell. However, that person would have ended up there eventually for rejecting salvation through Christ. It's their rejection of Christ—not the act of suicide—that condemns them.

Anyone who is in Christ is saved, has eternal life, and is forgiven by the blood of Jesus. An unsaved person who committed suicide would ultimately be in hell for rejecting salvation through Christ, no matter the cause of death—not because they committed suicide.

It's important to note that no one truly knows what happened in another person's heart at the moment they died. Some people have deathbed conversions and accept Christ in the final moments before death. It's possible that someone who committed suicide could have had a last-second change of heart and cried out for God's mercy. Others may curse God and send themselves to hell. We must leave such judgments to God. 1 Samuel 16:7 says, *"...for the Lord seeth not as man seeth; for man looketh on the outward appearance, but the Lord looketh on the heart."*

Many people struggle with despair. Our enemy, Satan, is a murderer from the beginning. John 8:44 says, *"Ye are of your father the devil, and the lusts of your father ye will do. He was a murderer from the beginning, and abode not in the truth, because there is no truth in him. When he speaketh a lie, he speaketh of his own: for he is a liar, and the father of it."* Suicide is never the answer to a problem, and it is a sin against God. According to the Bible, suicide is murder. But Jesus forgave us of *all* our sins, including suicide for those who are in Christ.

In the same manner, some religious hypocrites condemn me for my divorce or my tattoo because they look at the outward appearance. But the Lord looks at the heart. He knows those who believe. So, it's not right for someone to end their life, but it doesn't mean they are automatically condemned for it.

Christians are called to live their lives for God, and the decision of when to die is God's alone. The devil tries to convince both believers and non-believers alike to take their own lives—it is a part of his evil plans on the earth to steal, kill, and destroy people and their God-given destinies. If you have ever dealt with those thoughts, you're not alone, but I encourage you to call on the name of Jesus and remember He died and was resurrected, conquering death, to give you abundant life both on this earth and in heaven with Him. Everything is subject to the name of Jesus, including the spirit of suicide. Don't forget that God put you here with a destiny and a purpose and a good, expected end. Take refuge in Jesus and

God's Word. Seeing suicide as the solution to a problem is a deceptive trick of the devil. Don't fall for it. There is a better way. Call upon the name of Jesus!

Many people condemn my dad for what he did. I often share my testimony about his repentance. But even if I did not know of his repentance, I trust that God is in control of his soul—not some religious hypocrite like the Amish bishops who read a letter of condemnation over his grave. That's what religious people do.

"You'll be with me in paradise," Jesus said to the thief on the cross beside Him. He forgave him. Religious hypocrites crucified Jesus. Salvation has nothing to do with what we've done. It's all about grace alone, faith alone, and Christ alone. The thief who died beside Jesus that day was the first saved individual to enter paradise, and that's where my daddy is today. So, it doesn't matter what anyone says or how they twist the Word of God—I know I'm going to see my dad again. Who I won't see—unless they repent—are the religious hypocrites who condemned him and worship their traditions over God's truth.

59

MY SIBLINGS

I visited my twin brother, Levi, to share salvation with him. I was surprised to hear my Amish twin brother, in his New-Order Amish community in Huntingdon, Tennessee, tell me, "Eli, I'm saved too."

Astonished by what I'd heard, I asked, "You're what? Mom didn't want to hear the word salvation. She wanted nothing to do with trusting in grace alone, faith alone, and in Christ alone." I continued, "You're still Amish, and you're telling me you're saved? How can this be?"

My brother and his family attend Amish church every other Sunday. On Sundays the Amish bishops and elders would visit other districts to hold church, they went to the local English Baptist church because they spoke with power and authority. They prayed over people, and they were being set free. My brother was drawn to that, but he didn't see a reason to leave the Amish community. I practically leaped with joy over the news!

We still get together every year to celebrate our birthday, and on other occasions, too. We love to talk about Jesus when we get together. We can talk about the truth of God's Word. We even have Bible studies together. We have communion and break bread together because we're not just earthly brothers, we're also part of the body of Christ. Levi entered the sheepfold through the one door, Jesus the Christ. I was shocked that some of my family received it with joy.

Levi is the only one of my siblings who's saved so far. I visited my sister, Wilma, shortly after she got married. I didn't know who she had married, but when I arrived to see her, she met me at the front door. She said, "You're not welcome here. My kids will never see your face if you're not Amish."

I explained to Wilma, "Well, I just want to share what Christ has done for me."

"Whoa, whoa, whoa," she cut me off. She said, "You're of the world if you claim to be saved. You're using that as a pass to live in the world, to live in sin, and to drive a car. You know those things are going to send you to Hell."

"Have a good day," I said and left her to her ways.

I visited my oldest brother, Alvin. He was more open to letting me speak, but in the end, he still refused to believe that we can be saved by faith through grace.

"If you read the Bible and believe what you're reading, you can know that you're saved," I said. I shared 1 John 5:13 with him, and I said, "You can see right there in that verse. It says you can know that you are saved."

He retorted, "No, that's the Devil deceiving you."

"So, the Bible is written by the Devil. Is that what you're saying?" I asked.

"No, no, it's written by God. But if you read into it the way you do, or you do away with the Amish church ordinance and its rules, it's the Devil trying to deceive you away from our religion. We must stand firm even unto death," he said. "We're willing to die for our beliefs."

I told him, "Then you'll die in vain." I explained, "I'm willing to die for Jesus Christ. The Bible, the Word of God, the truth—that's what I'm willing to die for. But I'm not going to die for manmade rules and manmade religion. That's not going to get anyone to Heaven."

Each of my siblings had different responses to salvation. My mom had her reaction. My brother had his reaction. My sister had an extreme reaction by refusing to ever allow me back on her property. She made it clear that even if I were to wear Amish clothing like I did when visiting mom, she would never see me again.

When I visited my mom the next time, I shared with her that I didn't mean to make my sister Wilma angry. I showed up just to visit. I just wanted to love, honor, and chat with her. My mother explained that her father-in-law was a bishop. That piece of the puzzle explained everything. Her priority was impressing the elders and the bishop. She'd obtain brownie points and kudos for rejecting her worldly brother. Her motive is to be recognized, praised, and honored by men for rejecting me. Her actions weren't a result of some misguided devotion to God.

60

UNDECEPTION SPREADS

I recently heard from an Amish bishop who left the Amish community following his salvation. Many people are waking up to the truth. I regularly hear from members of the Amish community who reach out to me in frustration over their Amish ordinance and their communities' refusal to accept biblical truth. I also hear from other former Amish who have been out of the Amish community for a while. It's amazing to see and hear how many people are ministering and reaching back into the Amish culture to help set souls free.

Many receive salvation with joy in a tangible demonstration of Acts 2:17, *"In the last days, I will pour out my spirit on all flesh."* I'm convinced that is happening before our eyes. More Amish are leaving oppressive traditions than I've ever seen in my lifetime.

Others stand firm in their beliefs and are willing to die for their traditions; they have hardened their hearts. They believe that if they stand on those Amish traditions and do not waiver, God will give them credit. They have been blinded by the enemy and his deception. Their loyalty is misplaced, and their zeal for keeping rules is used to deceive them.

I was very excited to hear of an Amish bishop receiving salvation. He openly professed his faith and met with so much backlash from within his community that he finally said, "I'm out of here." He took his wife and left. Thank God his wife was on board because many times, when one spouse wants to leave, the other is not in agreement.

An Amish preacher in the Holmes County area told me the Amish church sent his wife to an Amish counseling facility because of his beliefs. He claimed to be saved by the blood of Jesus. He proclaimed he no longer believed in shunning. Because his beliefs went against the Amish church, his wife was sent to a counseling facility to avoid her being shunned. He decided to leave the Amish. Sadly, their marriage will probably end in divorce.

I was taught that divorce is an unforgivable sin. The Amish do not allow divorce. Even when a woman is being abused. But when their strict adherence to man-made theology and tradition divides marriages—they effectively force a divorce on people. That is about as alarming as it gets, but they don't see it. They're so firm in their traditions that they're willing to split a marriage and break up a family, all while believing God will credit them on judgment day.

Most people don't realize that the strict Old-Order communities will shun you for having a Bible study or claiming to understand salvation. To be fair, it's not that way in every Amish community. There is a movement toward biblical truth. Many New-Order Amish have reached out, asking me to not speak so harshly about the Amish. Many do believe in salvation, but they still adhere to an Amish ordinance. I often gently push back when they claim to believe in salvation and discover their community operates under an Ordnung.

An Ordnung church is German for communion Church. To be part of an Ordnung church, you must be perfectly aligned with the rules before taking communion. They believe that without communion you can't get into Heaven. Many New-Order Amish churches teach salvation in Christ and that it was finished at the cross, but by prioritizing strict rules not found in the Bible, they're still worshiping the Lord in vain. It doesn't matter how liberal your community is, just one man-made rule for salvation implies Jesus isn't good enough, and He didn't really finish the job. If you're placing your hope for justification and salvation in obeying a man-made rule, you don't believe the Bible; you aren't trusting in Jesus.

The Bible says in Ephesians 2:8-9, *"For by grace are ye saved through faith; and that not of yourselves: it is the gift of God: Not of works, lest any man should boast."* They want to boast. I'm delighted to hear when Amish people tell me they believe in salvation. It's a huge step in the right direction. But you don't really believe in something until you trust it fully. I pray for their complete undeception.

This is how religious systems deceive people. They speak the truth of the Bible, and then they add their own rules on top. Religion inserts itself between man and God and exercises control over people by convincing them that religion or tradition is necessary for them to enter Heaven and be acceptable to God. If people simply read their Bible, they'd find that the Bible speaks against religious systems. It stands to reason that many religious groups discourage or forbid people from reading the Bible to maintain control over them.

I heard from Amish preachers and bishops who told me how they found salvation, were freed from the veil of deception, and then immediately left their Amish community. If the Amish would actually read the Bible, they would see that they're guilty of the same thing the religious Pharisees did 2,000 years ago—the people who demanded the crucifixion of Christ. In Luke 6:22 (NIV), we read, *"Blessed are you, when people hate you, when they exclude you* (that's what's happening) *and insult you and reject your name as evil, because of the Son of Man."* That's what the Pharisees were doing at that time. If anybody professed Christ, they were cast out of the church as an evil person because they were no longer keeping the law of Moses. The Amish do the same—they cast people out as evil if they disobey their rules.

John 12:42-43 says this: *"Nevertheless among the chief rulers (the most religious Pharisees, the chief of them, chief rulers), also many believed on him; but because of the Pharisees, they did not confess Christ, lest they should be put out of the synagogue: for they loved the praise of men more than the praise of God."* Wow, did you catch that? "…they loved the praise of men more than the praise of God!" History is repeating itself today because people still choose to remain ignorant. That's why many remain in Amish communities; it's why many people remain within toxic religious systems and relationships. They find security in the approval of the forefathers and in the praise from the religious leaders.

If you persist in what you've always been told without seeking to know the truth, the truth can't set you free.

61

I DON'T HATE THE AMISH PEOPLE

If you've read this far and think I hate the Amish people, you've either missed my message or I haven't explained myself clearly.

The problem is not with the people themselves. Most Amish people are good-hearted, upright, honest, and care for their families and community. Most of them are moral people with great values. They make for great neighbors! Of course, there are some problems, as was the case in my family.

Just because I expose the heresy of the Amish church and their hypocrisy doesn't mean I believe the people lack good values. Their lifestyle is amazing. I enjoy their lifestyle more than any other culture in the world. Living off the land, self-sufficiency, and having no need for government—I love all that stuff. I could live the Amish lifestyle today. I love how they come together to help one another. The Amish community is the absolute best at helping one another when tragedies occur. When our barn burned down, it was rebuilt in three days. They have many good values, and the rest of the world should pay attention; it's not wrong to admire them for the things they do well. There's nothing wrong with living a simple life. But good values, high morals, and simple living won't get you into Heaven.

You are wise if you do business with the Amish. They make great products—better than the stuff made in China. You should absolutely buy Amish products and use their services. I still get Amish products, but because I'm shunned, I send my wife or others to get them. I still eat their baked goods. They don't know it's for me, but I still get it. They make some of the best quality log furniture, regular furniture, and crafts. Any furniture you buy from them will last you more than a lifetime. We bought a kitchen table from the Amish that cost almost three grand. I can promise you that my son, grandchildren, and great-grandchildren will be using that table long after I'm gone. I'm not joking. We had the same furniture throughout my entire childhood. Whatever the Amish make is strong, and they build it to endure; they do it the right way.

When I last visited Mom, I noticed the same chairs, table, and furniture as when I was two years old. She still has them. Never stop doing business with the Amish. They have some of the best products and make the best food.

Because I fear the Lord more than anything, I do what the Bible says: *"Love thy neighbor as thyself."* Even though I disagree with their theology and religion, I must give credit where credit is due. I love them because Jesus loves them. I must love my enemy, too. I love my family as best I can, even though they may say, "Hey, you're shunned. You can't come to my funeral." I still love them. I still get on my knees beside my bed every night and pray for my mom. I pray for those who slammed the door shut and said, "Don't come back. You're not welcome here for the rest of your life." I still get on my knees and shed tears over them. I ask the Lord, "Please forgive her. Father, she doesn't know what she's doing. Please forgive her." I plead for my mother's soul and the souls of my brothers and sisters, I pray that their eyes of understanding will be opened.

When I pray for those people and love them, I rest soundly at night. I have great peace. I wake up with a smile on my face and joy and peace in my heart. Because when Christ abides in you, and you abide in Him, you can do all things. You can rise above bitterness, anger, animosity, resentment, and hatred because all of that has been defeated by Jesus. Love defeats all these things. Love conquers the enemy. Love finished it at the cross. Love is the greatest command-ment from Jesus Himself. In John 13:34 (ESV), Jesus says, *"A new commandment I give to you, that you love one another: just as I have also loved you, you also are to love one another."*

If I have resentment, bitterness, anger, hatred, and unforgiveness toward somebody, the Bible says in Matthew 6:14-15, He can't forgive me if I don't forgive others. But if I forgive others, the Father in Heaven shall also forgive me. For that reason, I will always forgive. I can't do that in the flesh because my flesh wants to give knuckle sandwiches. If you haven't figure it out yet, Christ Jesus is the missing ingredient. You must have Jesus to conquer the enemy.

Jesus is the one who died without sin. He became sin for us and died on the cross. The Devil is defeated and has been stripped of all his power. When we are in Christ, *"Behold, I have given you authority to tread on serpents and scorpions, and over all the power of the enemy, and nothing shall hurt you"* (Luke 10:19 ESV). And *"you can do all things through Christ Jesus who strengthens you"* (Philippians 4:13). You can conquer the enemy, your sin, hatred, bitterness, addictions, habits, and whatever else that comes from your flesh.

The Devil has many people living in bondage, and they don't know it. What I love the most is sharing my testimony and experiences to help others become *undeceived*. I want people to be set free so they feel as though their whole body is above the water and no longer sinking, like Peter. Peter thought Jesus was a ghost when he saw Him walking on the water, and he was terrified (Matthew 14:25-31). He said, "Jesus, if that is You, tell me to come to You." And He said, "Come to me." Peter hopped out of the boat and started walking on water because of his faith. Then he looked at the storm. That's what many of us do when we make mistakes; we take our eyes off Jesus. We look at the storm, and we start sinking. Before you know it, you're in the water like Peter, yelling, "Oh Lord, help me. Lord, help me." We all do this at times. When you start sinking and you start doing things your own way and take your focus off Jesus, don't panic. Just say, "Lord, help me." He'll help you just as He did with Peter. He grabbed him out of the water, and He said, "Oh, you of little faith." Sometimes, I feel like I have little faith, but I always refocus on the Lord Jesus Christ.

That, my friends, is how you're going to get through the rest of this life until that great and glorious day when our mighty God and Savior Jesus Christ appears through those clouds.

62

WHAT ABOUT YOU?

I didn't know my life was going to play out the way it did, but God knew. That's not to say God caused everything that happened to me, but He used circumstances and situations for good that the Devil meant to destroy me. As a result, I have a powerful testimony, but it's really God's testimony. He was by my side before I even knew Him. If He did that for me, I promise He's by your side, no matter what you're going through. Maybe you've gone through worse things than what I've shared in this book. Just know that if God can rescue a crazy ex-Amish like me, He can also rescue you from all your storms, abuse, alcoholism, injustice, incarceration, or drug addiction. There's not an addiction, affliction, or circumstance on this Earth that He can't help you through. I know this because He helped me, and God is not a respecter of persons—what He does for one, He'll do for all.

My life circumstances were meant to keep me from coming to Christ and being delivered; the Devil wanted to kill me. But God used those circumstances for my good and then to benefit many others—my testimony has saved hundreds of people.

Even if you've never known Him, today, Jesus is right by your side. He knows your needs and all that you're going through. He knows about all your pain from childhood and throughout your life. He wants to take that pain from you, and He's just waiting for you to surrender it to Him. He can't take it from you until you know Him and are ready and willing to surrender it to Him. Stop relying on your own strength or man-made rules and systems. Jesus says, *"All of you who are weary and heavy laden, I will give you rest."* He gave me rest, and now He can give you rest, too.

If you have never considered Jesus as an option, do it today. Today is the day of salvation. Do not wait. He can give you peace and rest, even during very difficult situations. You can have the peace of Christ that surpasses all understanding and knowledge. He will give that to you, and it's a better high than anything you ever took to numb the pain in your life.

If I had not made that decision, I would be dead today. I'm convinced the Devil would have succeeded in destroying me. But God's mercy and grace saved me! Until I had faith in Jesus alone, I couldn't move forward in my life. You can make the same decision I did. You can live in peace, victory, joy, and happiness for the rest of your life until the day the Lord Jesus Christ comes through the clouds.

I want you to have a personal relationship with Jesus Christ; I want you to be saved. You might be reading this, and if you're honest, you can't pinpoint a time when you confessed your sin and declared your salvation. Maybe you're just not sure that you're saved. The good news is that you can take care of these matters today, right where you are, right now. If you are ready to receive Him, there is no doubt that you will.

Salvation starts with the confession of sin. First John 1:9 says, *"If we confess our sins, he is faithful and just to forgive us our sins and cleanse us from all unrighteousness."* Sometimes, when people hear the word "confession," they envision telling all their sins to a priest, bishop, or elders of the church. They think someone needs to pass judgment on their confession and essentially forgive them on behalf of God. I want you to know that this is not true. You can confess your sin directly to Jesus, who's by your side waiting. He can hear you, and He already did everything necessary to forgive you when He died on the cross; He's simply waiting for you to believe, confess, and receive your forgiveness by faith.

Jesus also wants you to forgive yourself. I made my confession to Jesus, and I knew I was forgiven because I believed through faith that Jesus died on the cross, was buried, and rose again on the third day. I have eternal life because of what He did. Praise God! Don't be like me and cling to your sin, unable to forgive yourself. Jesus finished the job on the cross and now you are free to let go of your sin. Jesus forgives you; now you can forgive yourself.

You can pray a very simple prayer from your heart. Talk to Jesus just as you would a person sitting beside you. You can say something like:

Jesus, I recognize that I am a sinner and I need Your forgiveness. I believe You died for my sins, and You rose from the grave to give me eternal life. I surrender my life to You now, and I receive Your forgiveness. Please help me to follow You all the days of my life. Thank You for Your love and grace. In Jesus' name, amen.

Romans 10:9 (NIV) says, *"If you declare with your mouth, 'Jesus is Lord,' and believe in your heart that God raised him from the dead, you will be saved."* It is very important that you open your mouth and tell someone about your decision to follow Christ. This is what it means to declare with your mouth. Tell someone you trust. I told my wife. I knew she had been praying for me, so she was the one I wanted to tell. But you need to open your mouth and tell someone; you can't keep it a secret.

I can't overemphasize the importance of reading the Bible every day. Once you have made your confession to Jesus and declared your faith to someone you trust, you must get into the Word of God and start feeding on the Word. If you need a place to start, begin with the Book of John. Read it several times. The Book of John is all about Jesus, which makes it an excellent starting place. The New Testament will help you understand Jesus, the true meaning of salvation, and what it's like to live a Christian life. You need to read the whole New Testament. Don't be tempted to just read a few verses haphazardly, as is the practice of some people. You need to get the whole of God's Word into your spirit. Each of the books has its own unique message, and you need every part.

After reading the Book of John, I read the entire New Testament multiple times, and I highly recommend you do it too. Read it through, then start over again. Every time you read it, more and more revelation is released into your spirit. Think of it like medicine; just keep taking it every day.

The Book of Acts talks a lot about the Holy Spirit and His function in our lives. I felt the power and presence of the Holy Spirit strongly when reading the Book of Acts. It caused me to weep with joy. Each book has its own theme and message. It's important to pray about what you read because the Lord can put a particular book in your heart. Always pray before reading the Word and ask for the Holy Spirit's guidance.

I'm not discounting the Old Testament. You'll want to read that too, but it'll make more sense if you have a good foundation in the New Testament. The Old Testament speaks of Jesus, but that's hard to see if you haven't read the New Testament first. The Old Testament teaches about the nature of God. But if you're just getting started, get a good handle on the New Testament first.

As you pray, ask the Holy Spirit to lead you to a church gathering. I go to a non-denominational church that is important to me. It helps me grow, learn from others, pray with and for others, and encourage others. "Iron sharpens iron," the Bible says. Churches are places where iron sharpens iron on a Sunday morning if people first read the Bible, discover the truth, become born again (saved), and let the Holy Spirit lead them into all truth. That's why I simply share the Gospel and encourage people to get into reading God's Word. The Holy Spirit does the rest.

The Holy Spirit will lead you to a gathering of believers, and you must seek a relationship with a group of genuine, committed believers—people who passionately and wholeheartedly worship and serve God. Depending on where you live, you might need to drive a distance to find the kind of church I described. Not all churches are the same. Many are simply gatherings where people affirm each other in whatever they want to do; they simply pat each other on the back. This is NOT iron sharpening iron. Other churches are cults seeking power and money at your expense; they have seemingly endless rules and rituals that complicate the simple Gospel of Jesus and seek to insert themselves between you and God; stay away from such places.

When I first got saved, I didn't want to gather. I had no desire to be around those people. I just wanted to read the Word for myself. I figured I could worship the Lord by myself. But the Holy Spirit kept giving me a desire and a will to fellowship with other believers. Just like I used to have a will to party with others who enjoyed sinning, now I seek the company of other believers. And while we don't call it "partying," that's sort of what we do, except we choose to call it fellowship. Fellowship is a church word, but it's not that different from partying, except it's deeper and much more satisfying. It helps that it doesn't leave you with a headache or memory loss; you actually feel great!

Allow the Holy Spirit to lead you. If He has a plan for you to be in ministry, He will guide you. God has a plan and a will for everyone's life. It's not God's will for any to perish. That is why God wanted me to start my ministry when I got saved in that semi-truck. I became the "Preaching Truck Driver" right then and there.

God can take you places, too. He'll use you in amazing ways and satisfy you in ways you never imagined. Living water is incredible, but you need to reject religion and begin with His Word.

AFTERWORD

If this book has impacted you in some way, I'd like to hear from you. If you've decided to surrender your life to Jesus and live undeceived, please let me know by going to www.eliyoder.com/justgot saved. I want to send you encouragement to help you get started.

Please tell me how my story has impacted you or share your comments about the book by going to www.eliyoder.com/sharemys tory. This will encourage me and help me minister to you and others in the future.

You can also join my email list by going to www.eliyoder.com/email so we can keep in touch in the future.

May God bless you fully and richly, and may you walk undeceived all your days!

ABOUT THE AUTHOR

Eli Yoder grew up in an Old-Order Amish community in Hardin County, Ohio. At eighteen, Eli left the community after facing condemnation for riding a bicycle—an experience that characterized the oppressive traditions of his upbringing. His departure marked the beginning of a journey to discover truth and freedom through the Bible and salvation in Jesus Christ.

Now residing in Waynesfield, Ohio, with his wife Nikki and their son Johnathan, Eli is a passionate preacher, truck driver, and social media personality. Known as "the preaching truck driver," Eli shares straightforward and heartfelt messages from the cab of his truck through social media, where he discusses Bible teachings and his life experiences both within and outside the Amish community. His mission extends beyond his own story—Eli frequently supports former Amish individuals, helping them transition into mainstream society by offering guidance and resources.

In 2017, Eli experienced a life-changing encounter with Jesus. This moment marked a turning point in his life and cemented his commitment to sharing the truth of God's Word. Through his online platforms, Eli passionately brings the message of freedom from spiritual oppression, helping others break free from the deceptions of man-made religious traditions. Eli also travels to various churches around the country, sharing his testimony and message of freedom from religious legalism while abiding in Jesus.

Eli's message is not only about leaving a way of life, but also about finding a path illuminated by the truth of Jesus. His work sheds light on the complexities and challenges of the Amish, making him an influential voice in discussions about religious oppression and personal autonomy.

On a lighter note, Eli is a passionate Ohio State Buckeyes fan. He often jokes, "If it wasn't for Jesus and Ohio State football, it might not have been worth it to leave the Amish Egypt!"

Visit: eliyoder.com
Join Eli's Mailing List: eliyoder.com/email
Share Your Story Or Comment: eliyoder.com/sharemystory
Just Got Saved? Tell Eli: eliyoder.com/justgotsaved

facebook.com/eli.yoder.33
instagram.com/eliyoder2024
youtube.com/@eliyoder491
tiktok.com/@yodertoter40

Printed in the USA
CPSIA information can be obtained
at www.ICGtesting.com
CBHW030045271024
16410CB00004B/100